Derek Rowntree has wor
both managing and being managed, and is now Professor of
Educational Development in the Open University. His chief
interest is in staff development and vocational training —
especially through the medium of open learning. In addition
to his consultancy work and writings in these fields, he is
also the author of a number of popular paperbacks such as
Statistics Without Tears (Penguin), *The Manager's Book of
Checklists* (Corgi) and *Learn How to Study* (Warner).

Also available by Derek Rowntree:

LEARN HOW TO STUDY
TEACH YOURSELF WITH OPEN LEARNING

HOW TO MANAGE
YOUR BOSS
~ and survive the system

Derek Rowntree

WARNER BOOKS

A *Warner* Book

First published in Great Britain by Sphere Books Ltd 1989
Reprinted 1991
Reprinted by Warner Books 1993

Typeset by Selectmove Ltd, London
Printed in England by Clays Ltd, St Ives plc

ISBN 0 7515 0725 3

Warner Books
A Division of
Little, Brown and Company (UK) Ltd
165 Great Dover Street
London SE1 4YA

Contents

Chapter 1

Why Bosses Need Managing

Benjamin Franklin said there is nothing certain in this world except death and taxes. But he should also have mentioned bosses. There's no escaping them. Everybody's got a boss.

I don't know about you, but I've been through quite a lot of them in my time. On the buses and in hospitals, in factories and offices, in hotels and the civil service, and in schools, colleges and universities. At the time, they all seemed very different. Looking back to them, however, I am now more conscious of what they had in common.

Bosses are no doubt as varied and individual as the rest of us. But when you come down to it, there are just three basic types – the good ones, the so-so ones, and the bad ones. The good ones are those who help you get the best out of your job. The so-so ones are maybe not particularly helpful but at least they usually manage to avoid getting in your way. And, of course, the bad ones can make your working life a hell on earth.

We don't normally have much choice as to which type we get landed with. But there's a lot we can do to encourage the good boss, to make the so-so one better, and to make a bad one less bad. This is the art and craft of boss-management.

Now there are plenty of courses and books for managers on how to manage. But nobody bothers to tell the 'poor bloody workers' how to survive being managed. Hence this book. It is meant for people who aren't prepared just to sit back and let things happen to them. It is for people who are ready to take responsibility for their own fates and make sure they don't get exploited or overlooked.

MANAGING BEING MANAGED

It's a boss's job to manage your work. But if you want to survive being managed, you need to manage your bosses. To manage your bosses means getting them to:

- Notice you
- Respect you
- Acknowledge your strengths
- Rely on you
- Allow you to influence their decisions
- Help you progress towards your own goals
- Make your working life tolerable/productive for you
- Keep you out of messes
- Avoid getting in your way or making a fool of you

In short, it means influencing the way they *see* you and *behave* towards you. Managing your boss is the only way to stop the system grinding you down.

There are five main aspects to this:

1. Capture your boss's attention.
2. Convince them of the benefit of having your support.
3. Prove the benefit, e.g. by doing a good job.
4. Make them fear losing that benefit.
5. Extract your 'price' for continuing to provide it.

PROBLEMS WITH BOSSES

One of the commonest causes of stress and unhappiness at work is problems with the boss. Since I started looking into this subject, people have told me of quite a variety. Here are some of them. Tick any that sound like problems you have (or perhaps not, if you'd rather not risk your boss seeing your answers):

A. 'I'm not sure who my real boss is.'   [ ]
B. 'I hardly ever see my boss.'   [ ]
C. 'My boss won't leave me to get on with the job.'   [ ]
D. 'My boss keeps me in the dark about what I am supposed to be doing or achieving.'   [ ]
E. 'My boss can't seem to make up her mind about what she expects from me.'   [ ]
F. 'My boss makes decisions that affect the work of my staff without consulting me.'   [ ]
G. 'My boss used to do my job and finds it difficult to accept that I want to do it differently.'   [ ]
H. 'My boss is too busy currying favour with superiors to bother with rank-and-filers like me.'   [ ]
I. 'My boss is never around when there's trouble.'   [ ]
J. 'My boss has his drinking cronies and if you're not one of them, you're nobody.'   [ ]
K. 'My boss is weak and doesn't fight for what our department needs.'   [ ]
L. 'My boss doesn't give my ideas the encouragement I believe they deserve.'   [ ]
M. 'My boss is always quick to criticize "keeping us on our toes" but rarely gives praise.'   [ ]
N. 'My boss is too worried about us making mistakes and drawing down the wrath of the powers-that-be to risk doing anything innovative.'   [ ]
O. 'My boss doesn't delegate properly.'   [ ]
P. 'My boss is pig-headed, domineering, and liable to get violent (verbally if not physically).'   [ ]
Q. 'My boss can't keep his hands to himself.'   [ ]

You may have one or more of the above problems. Or you may have a completely different set of problems all your own. From my own experience, I would add the bosses who've told me – either by their words or by their actions:

- 'Don't ask questions.'
- 'Don't think.'
- 'Don't try to understand.'
- 'Just do as you're told'
- 'Leave the decisions to me.'
- 'I'll see you right.'
- 'Check everything with me first.'

WHAT ARE THE CAUSES?

Whatever your boss-problems, you are likely to find they have one or more of three basic causes:

1. The organization
2. The person who is your boss
3. You

Maybe your organization is one where you'd be *bound* to have trouble with your boss. No matter who filled that post, he or she would be likely to act in much the same way. Suppose, for example, your boss doesn't tell you as much as you think you should be told about what is going on. This may be because you work in a secretive sort of organization where even your boss doesn't get told much.

But maybe not. Maybe the problem arises purely because of the particular individual – their personality, or beliefs, or preferred style of managing. (Perhaps your boss is just the uncommunicative type.)

Then again, could the problem arise because of something *you* are doing – or not doing? If you are to have any hope of overcoming problems, then you'd better believe it. You probably can't get your manager changed, and you've even less chance of getting the whole organization to change its ways. But *you* can do things differently. That's what this book is all about. You can get more of what you want from work if you learn to manage your boss. (Maybe you've never told your uncommunicative boss what it is you want to know more about.)

In this book, we'll be looking at at all three aspects – you, your organization and your boss – and how you all interact. But let's start with you . . .

WHAT DO YOU WANT FROM YOUR WORK?

If you hadn't wanted more control over your work situation, I doubt if you'd have picked up this book at all. But why do you want more control? For what purpose? Perhaps you are hoping to get something from your work situation that you are not getting at present. Or maybe you are just hoping to hang onto something that you fear may be taken away from you.

Either way, it raises the question of what you want from your work. And this depends on what you want from your life as a whole. Your work may be a great source of satisfaction to you – perhaps the most important thing in your life. You may be one of those who 'live to work'.

On the other hand, your work may be just what you do to pay the bills. You may 'work to live' and if you suddenly inherited a fortune you would give up the job tomorrow.

Few of us ever spend much time thinking about what we want from work. Fewer still consider what we might want from life. Most of us just muddle through both our careers and our lives. Then, quite suddenly, both are almost over and we realize it is too late to achieve our true desires.

Taking Stock
Those of us who do take stock occasionally, and consider seriously what they really desire (and whether they are prepared to pay the price), are the wise ones. And all it needs is the determination to ask ourselves a few simple questions, to be honest in our answers, and to follow through with appropriate action.

For instance, ask yourself:

- What have been the most satisfying things that have happened in my life so far?
- What have been the most satisfying things that have happened in my career?
- Are there similarities among the things that have given me satisfaction?
- Can I see ways of obtaining similar satisfactions in future?
- What youthful aspirations have I not yet fulfilled?
- Do I still want to fulfil them?
- Are there any newer aspirations I want to fulfil?
- How many years do I think I might have left to me?
- What is the best way of using them?

It's worth asking yourself such questions at regular intervals – at least once a year, and additionally whenever you are considering a change of job. They all have a bearing on how (and why) you might manage your boss.

What Do You Want From Life?
We all of us want different things from life. Some of those things we can get from our work, if we play our cards right. Others are only obtainable only outside work – from family, friends, sports, hobbies, community activity, and so on.

Consider the following possible life aims. Pick out the five that seem most important to you, and rank those five from most important (1) to least important (5):

- To make as much money as possible   [ ]
- To help people less fortunate than I am   [ ]
- To enjoy love and/or companionship   [ ]
- To have a secure and untroubled life   [ ]
- To have power over other people   [ ]
- To become as famous as possible   [ ]
- To be a successful parent and partner to my spouse   [ ]
- To become an acknowledged expert   [ ]
- To make worthwhile things or provide a valued service   [ ]

- To be free of other people's demands   [ ]
- To have an exciting, adventurous (perhaps risky) life   [ ]
- To do what I believe to be my duty   [ ]
- To indulge myself, having as much pleasure as possible   [ ]
- To feel I have fulfilled my potential   [ ]
- Others (what?)   . . .

How Does Your Work Tie In?

Now think about your work in terms of the five chief life aims you picked out above. How far do they tie in to your present job?

- Which (if any) of your five aims are you attaining through your present job?

- If there are any you are not attaining at present, can you imagine how you might be able to attain them through your work – e.g. by managing your boss better?

- If there are some you couldn't expect to attain through your present job, do you know of some other line of work in which you could expect to attain them?

- If you see no way of pursuing your five key aims through your work, does it matter? (Perhaps you are satisfying them quite happily in your life outside work.)

- But does your work actively hinder you in pursuing your most important life aims?

Possible Changes

I wonder if the questions above help you identify any changes you might want to make in your job or your life. You might ask yourself what you would you hope to be doing one year from now – and five years from now – to get more in line with your main life aims. Perhaps you can see a sequence of steps you need to take in order to achieve these goals.

You may be able to identify advantages and strengths you

have that should help you to take those steps. But maybe you also have weaknesses or disadvantages (e.g. your boss) that you will need to overcome or find some way around. How might you need to develop your abilities?

And what sacrifices might you need to make in order to reach your goal? Trying to attain some of your life aims might mean that you need to abandon others. For instance, a cosy family life is not easily attained by the workaholic. And it's difficult to sustain close friendships with your colleagues at work if your main aim is to rise above them in the hierarchy. Only you can decide which sacrifices are worthwhile, and how far you may want to modify your goals.

WHAT DO YOU WANT NOW?

So much for the long term. Let's come back to the present. Let's consider what you are looking for from your present job.

Here are a number of possible satisfactions that different people get from their work. Pick out, say, five that are important to you and which you would like to get more of – perhaps by managing your boss better:

- Increasing wages or salary [ ]
- Regular promotions [ ]
- Official fringe benefits ('perks') [ ]
- Unofficial fringe benefits [ ]
- Plenty of time off work [ ]
- Turning out high quality work [ ]
- Being able to learn new skills [ ]
- The easy life of undemanding routine work [ ]
- The challenge of changing, variable work [ ]
- Contributing to a worthwhile enterprise [ ]
- Gaining personal status or power [ ]
- Agreeable working conditions [ ]
- Being told exactly what to do [ ]
- Practising and improving my expertise [ ]
- Having some freedom to decide how I work [ ]

- The feeling of being needed   [ ]
- Social relationships with colleagues   [ ]
- Being respected within the organization   [ ]
- Being respected by outsiders   [ ]
- Others (what?)   . . .

KNOW YOUR PRIORITIES

Each of us will feel differently about the items in a list like this. But the answers you choose should paint a fair picture of what your priorities are and why you might need to manage your boss.

Maybe your aim in managing your boss is to win promotion, power and high earnings. Maybe it's more to do with getting his or her support so that you can go on getting better and better at what you already do well and get satisfaction from. Or perhaps you are quite happy with the way things are and you want to resist any pressure from your boss to aim higher than you want to go. Only you will know.

But if you want to manage your boss and survive within your organization, you'll need to keep your aims in mind. It is easy to get side-tracked with offers (or threats) you feel you can't ignore, but probably can.

In the next chapter, we'll look at the organization within which you and your boss are working. As you will realize, the nature of that organization has a lot to do with how your boss manages you and how far you might be able to achieve your aims.

Chapter 2

Know Your Organization

How well do you understand the organization you work in? The more you know about it, the better you'll understand where you and your boss fit in. So you'll be in a better position to manage your boss and survive the organization.

No two organization are the same. Working in a civil service department is quite different from working in one of a chain of retail stores. And this is quite different again from working in a hospital or a television company or a car factory.

Different organizations have different ways of doing things. So, too, may different departments or sections within the same organizations. And they have different expectations of the people who work in them. For instance, you may or may not be expected to call your boss by his or her first name. You may be expected to wear formal clothes at work, or you may be expected to dress casually.

And, at a deeper level, you and your colleagues may have strongly-held beliefs about the organization and about how you expect one another to do things. These beliefs may not be immediately apparent to outsiders. But they will be different from the beliefs held by people in other organizations. They will help mark out what is distinctive about life in your organization – and in your section in particular.

WHAT'S YOUR LOCAL CULTURE?

So what is *distinctive* about the organization you work in?
Many different words have been used to refer to this distinctive 'feel' that each organization has – its 'climate', its
'personality', its 'ethos', its 'culture'.

Whatever the word, it means that you couldn't expect to
go from working in, say, an oil refinery or the armed services
to working in, say, an advertising agency or a computer software company and expect to relate in the same way to people
elsewhere in the organization. The distinctive 'culture' of
your organization will make its own demands on both you
and your boss. It may offer unique opportunities but at the
same time it will set unique limits to what is possible. You
ignore it at your peril.

WHAT ARE THE ORGANIZATION'S GOALS?

One way of understanding an organizations is to ask what its
goals appear to be. What do people emphasize when they're
talking to one another? And what seems to be the point of
their daily activities?

Look at each of the following possible goals. Ask yourself,
first of all, which of them are emphasized by your organization in general (Org.). Then ask yourself which of them are
emphasized within your section (Sec.). Tick as many as seem
relevant.

	Org.	Sec.
• Increasing productivity	[ ]	[ ]
• Cutting costs	[ ]	[ ]
• Increasing share of market	[ ]	[ ]
• Increasing profits	[ ]	[ ]
• Good public relations	[ ]	[ ]
• Keeping up traditions	[ ]	[ ]
• Introducing new products/methods	[ ]	[ ]

- Employee satisfaction   [ ]   [ ]
- Responding to clients'/customers' needs   [ ]   [ ]
- Avoiding outside interference   [ ]   [ ]
- Others (which?)   . . .   . . .

You may have decided that the goals in your section are very similar to those of the organization as a whole. You may have decided they are rather different. Or you may have decided that the goals at both levels are too vague for you to be sure about.

It will help you to be at least as clear as your boss is about what the goals are. You may need to convince him or her that (despite appearances perhaps) what you are doing is helping to achieve them!

YOUR ORGANIZATION'S SELF-IMAGE

How do people *feel* about your organization and about working in it? Which of the following phrases best reflect people's feelings? Again, consider first the organization generally, and then your own section. Tick as many as you think relevant.

	Org.	Sec.
- Go-getting and ruthlessly efficient	[ ]	[ ]
- Warm, friendly and relaxed	[ ]	[ ]
- Cold, rife with conflicts and stressful	[ ]	[ ]
- Making a worthwhile contribution to society	[ ]	[ ]
- Carrying on a proud tradition	[ ]	[ ]
- Expanding and optimistic	[ ]	[ ]
- Defensive and pessimistic	[ ]	[ ]
- Innovative and exciting	[ ]	[ ]
- Old-fashioned and complacent	[ ]	[ ]
- Encouraging of individual initiative	[ ]	[ ]
- Stifled by red tape and heavy management	[ ]	[ ]
- A good outfit to work in	[ ]	[ ]
- OK, but not what it used to be	[ ]	[ ]

- Getting better all the time   [ ]   [ ]
- The ship is definitely sinking   [ ]   [ ]
- Others (which?)   . . .   . . .

Keeping abreast of how other people feel about the organization is essential if you are to get on well within it. Don't assume that people in other sections necessarily feel the same way as people in yours. Indeed there may be differences of opinion even within your section.

Clearly, you especially need to know what your boss's feelings are – and how they may differ from yours.

THE PACE OF WORK

Are you working towards some distant target, or does each day present a target of its own? Is your working life leisurely or are you rushed off your feet? Organizations differ greatly in how far their staff must look ahead, and in the speed at which they need to work. So do sections within them. How does this apply to your organization generally and to your section in particular?

	Org.	Sec.
How far ahead do work targets extend?		
– Hours	[ ]	[ ]
– Days	[ ]	[ ]
– Weeks	[ ]	[ ]
– Months	[ ]	[ ]
– Years	[ ]	[ ]
How would you describe the pace of work?		
– Lethargic and apathetic	[ ]	[ ]
– Slow but steady	[ ]	[ ]
– Busy but rarely over-stretched	[ ]	[ ]
– Sometimes slow/sometimes frantic	[ ]	[ ]
– Staggering from crisis to crisis	[ ]	[ ]
– So frantic or erratic as to be inefficient	[ ]	[ ]
– Other (what?)	. . .	. . .

Are you happy with the pace of work in your section? If not, maybe it's one of the things about which you'll want to influence your boss – especially if your section seems to be out of line with the rest of the organization.

WHO HAS INFLUENCE?

Whatever it is you want from your job, many people may have some influence over the extent to which you get it. The 'quality of working life' may be affected by the views such people express and the actions they take.

Which of the following people in your organization express views or take actions that have a *noticeable* influence on the satisfactions people can get from their work? Tick as many as you think necessary.

	Org.	Sec.
• Individual employees	[ ]	[ ]
• Groups of employees	[ ]	[ ]
• Line managers and supervisors	[ ]	[ ]
• Staff specialists (e.g. in personnel or accounts)	[ ]	[ ]
• Outside consultants	[ ]	[ ]
• Directors	[ ]	[ ]
• Shareholders	[ ]	[ ]
• Customers/clients	[ ]	[ ]
• Suppliers	[ ]	[ ]
• Trade unions	[ ]	[ ]
• Government	[ ]	[ ]
• Outside pressure groups	[ ]	[ ]
• Others (which?)	. . .	. . .

You may have noticed that people other than managers and supervisors can have influence on people's work in your organization or in your section. You may need to bear this in mind in trying to manage your boss. These other people may need 'managing' too.

In some cases, you may decide that the best way to achieve your goals may be to get support from someone *other* than your boss – e.g. an outside consultant or a group of your colleagues. Effective boss-management may call for teamwork.

MANAGEMENT STYLES

There are many ways of managing people. Modern management training emphasises very different styles from those of twenty or thirty years ago.

But most managers have had little or no training. Their own management style is usually just a personal variation on the way they themselves were or are managed. There are still large differences in style between different organizations and, to a lesser extent, between one section of an organization and another.

Which of the following phrases best describe the most typical styles of management in your organization and in your section? Tick as many as seem relevant.

	Org.	Sec.
• Bureaucratic, formal and 'by the book'	[ ]	[ ]
• Informal, flexible and 'human'	[ ]	[ ]
• Consultative and encouraging participation	[ ]	[ ]
• Authoritarian and directive	[ ]	[ ]
• Concerned primarily with getting the job done	[ ]	[ ]
• Concerned primarily with helping people develop	[ ]	[ ]
• About equally concerned with the job and people	[ ]	[ ]
• Over-demanding and exploitative	[ ]	[ ]
• Demanding but reasonable	[ ]	[ ]
• Ill-informed and autocratic	[ ]	[ ]
• Supportive and stimulating	[ ]	[ ]
• Paternalistic and patronizing	[ ]	[ ]
• Others (what?)	. . .	. . .

Did you recognize your local style among the phrases I mentioned? Maybe there is more than one style on the loose in your organization. If so, might this make things easier or more difficult if you and your colleagues wanted to encourage your boss to change his or her style?

And what sort of style do you prefer, anyway? (More of this when we get to thinking about your boss in the next chapter.)

HUMAN RELATIONSHIPS

Management style has a considerable effect on the relationships that staff have amongst themselves. I've worked in one organization, for instance, where the section supervisor prohibited talking in the office – just like in school. So people came in, did their work, and went home. To all intents and purposes, they had no relationships. They didn't chat socially and they didn't routinely share information about their work either.

Organizations differ greatly in the kinds of relationships they produce among their staff – making the place more, or less, congenial (and possibly more, or less, productive) to work in.

What are relationships within your organization and your section like? Does it strike you, in general, that people:

	Org.	Sec.
• Have common goals	[ ]	[ ]
or have conflicting goals?	[ ]	[ ]
• Share common beliefs	[ ]	[ ]
or disagree on important matters?	[ ]	[ ]
• Trust one another	[ ]	[ ]
or suspect/fear one another?	[ ]	[ ]
• Help one another out with work problems	[ ]	[ ]
or refrain from helping one another?	[ ]	[ ]
• Protect one another's interests	[ ]	[ ]
or try to gain at one another's expense?	[ ]	[ ]

- Take pride in one another's work   [ ]   [ ]
  or ignore/rubbish one another's work?   [ ]   [ ]
- Exchange personal confidences   [ ]   [ ]
  or keep themselves to themselves?   [ ]   [ ]
- Meet outside work   [ ]   [ ]
  or avoid each other outside work?   [ ]   [ ]
- Any other positive features (what?)   [ ]   [ ]
  or negative features (what?)   [ ]   [ ]

I expect you will be less clear about relationships elsewhere in your organization than you are about those in your own section. It may have crossed your mind, however, that relationships in your section are rather different from those in certain other sections you know of. And you may be aware that relationships between staff in your section and staff in other sections are not always as positive as they might be. Such thoughts may or may not have a bearing on what you might want to get out of your job – and how you might want to manage your boss.

THE COMMUNICATION PATTERN

Communication, or the lack of it, has a big influence on our life at work. Some people say 'They never tell us anything,' while others say 'At least everybody here knows what's going on.'

How would you describe the general style of communication within your organization and section? Tick as many as seem to apply.

	Org.	Sec.
• Candid and open	[ ]	[ ]
• Tightly controlled	[ ]	[ ]
• Haphazard	[ ]	[ ]
• Purposely evasive or misleading	[ ]	[ ]
• Grapevine very important	[ ]	[ ]
• Poor communication down from bosses	[ ]	[ ]

- Good communication down from bosses   [ ]   [ ]
- Poor communication upwards   [ ]   [ ]
- Good communication upwards   [ ]   [ ]
- Poor communication between sections   [ ]   [ ]
- Good communication between sections   [ ]   [ ]
- Communication is generally:
  - reliable   [ ]   [ ]
  - unreliable   [ ]   [ ]
  - helpful/supportive   [ ]   [ ]
  - critical/discouraging   [ ]   [ ]
- Others (what?)   . . .   . . .

It's difficult to make the most of your situation unless you
are told or can find out what's going on. Your boss *may* be
a source of the information you need to make sensible decisions. But very often your boss will be as much in the dark as
you are. You may need to cultivate the informal grapevine.
There is always someone who really knows what the score is
– e.g. your boss's boss's secretary or the caretaker.

WHO DOES WELL?

No-one who wants to survive and prosper within an organization can afford to ignore this key question. What kinds of
people get on well – in terms of whatever it is they want out
of work – in your organization and in your section? Think
of colleagues who seem to have got what they were most
looking for from the system – whether money, power, new
skills, companionship, or whatever. Tick whichever of the
following items you think describe them.

	Org.	Sec.
The people who get what they want are those who:		
• Are technically competent and work hard	[ ]	[ ]
• Produce more than others	[ ]	[ ]
• Suck up to the bosses	[ ]	[ ]

- Show loyalty 'beyond the call of duty'   [ ]   [ ]
- Avoid making trouble for management   [ ]   [ ]
- Stick meticulously to the rules   [ ]   [ ]
- Look after their own interests   [ ]   [ ]
- Seek power and manipulate others   [ ]   [ ]
- Help others to develop   [ ]   [ ]
- Generate useful ideas   [ ]   [ ]
- Don't try to set themselves above others   [ ]   [ ]
- Earn the respect of colleagues   [ ]   [ ]
- Earn the respect of people outside   [ ]   [ ]
- Others (what?)   . . . . . .

Did you find it easy to see what qualities help people get on within your section and your organization? Are any of them qualities you have yourself? If not, do you think you might want to develop any of them in order to achieve your aims? Do you think you would be able to?

If you are to manage your boss you will need to know what qualities she or he seems to be looking for in individuals. Only then can you present yourself to best advantage.

WHAT ARE THE IMPLICATIONS FOR YOU?

We have already considered a number of facets of organizational life. Maybe your organization has yet other facets worth thinking about in the same sort of way? I asked you to tick the best descriptions of how things are in your organization generally and in your section in particular:

a) Did you usually find you were ticking the same items for both? If so, the 'climate' or 'culture' in your section is presumably pretty similar to that in the organization as a whole. This would suggest that you and your colleagues are probably well integrated with the rest of the organization and don't have too much trouble relating to other sections.

b) But what if your ticks didn't match up too well? This would suggest that your section is to some extent at odds with the culture of the organization. Do you think this is so? Does it cause you problems? Does anything need to be done about it? (If so, can you do anything – perhaps by working on your boss – to make things better?)

c) Thinking about these various aspects of the organization may also have led you to think about your own preferences. You may have a clearer picture of how things are within your organization and section. But how far does this match up with the way you'd like them to be?

You may be generally satisfied with things within your section, but feel your section is at odds with the organization as a whole. This may present you with problems, especially if you are trying to get your boss to do something for you within the rest of the organization – e.g. arranging training for you in another section.

On the other hand, you may feel envious of certain ways of doing things that are common elsewhere in the organization but not in your section. If so, you may want to put them on your agenda for managing the boss. Or, of course, you may plan to transfer to another, more congenial, section.

And what if you don't like the way things are done either within your section *or* within the organization as a whole? Then you really do have a problem. You may decide that no amount of boss-management is going to make a worthwhile difference if the whole organizational culture is against it. Maybe you'll decide you might be happier in a different kind of organization altogether.

Knowing your organization is a vital element in controlling your destiny. Which aspects of such knowledge you need will depend on what you are trying to achieve. But it is important to keep your knowledge of the organizational culture up to date.

Organizations don't stand still. So cultures change. If you've ever been involved in a takeover or merger, you'll probably know this only too well. New owners, new bosses, new technology, new government policy – any of them drag an organization kicking and screaming into new ways of doing things (maybe even doing different things) practically overnight. The advantage goes to those people who see such changes coming.

KNOWING YOUR OWN TEAM

To finish this chapter, let's consider those members of your organization you work most closely with every day. They may be what you've been thinking of as your 'section'. Or they may be a smaller group *within* your section. Let's call them your 'team'.

Whether you work closely with everyone in your section or with just a few people within it, there are several things worth knowing about your team. For instance:

- Is your team well-regarded by other sections of the organization?

- What determines how your team is regarded by the rest of the organization?

- Does your team have any rivals or enemies?

- Does your team have *official* working relationships with other teams?

- Do individuals have close *informal* relationships with individuals in other teams?

- Can they obtain advance warning about changes likely to affect your team?

- Who manages the work of the team?

- How is the boss regarded by the team?

- How is he or she regarded by people outside the team?

- Which of your colleagues do you feel you could most rely on to help you out of a tight spot?

- Do you have any colleagues you can confide in and share ideas with?

- Are there any colleagues you couldn't trust?

- **Are there any colleagues with whom you might be able to collaborate in managing your boss?**

That last question is a crucial one. Two or more minds (and will-powers) may sometimes be better than one when it comes to moving the boss. Your individual efforts may get you nowhere unless your colleagues back you. Indeed, they may even try to sabotage your efforts if they think you are trying to get yourself some advantage over them. Group solidarity will often be a powerful tool in managing the boss. It's as well to know who your allies are – both within your section and outside it.

Chapter 3

Know Your Boss

Who is your boss? This may seem like a daft question. Everybody knows who their boss is, don't they? Well, not always. For one thing, some people have more than one boss. I can think of a group of secretaries, for instance, each of whom not only has more than one manager to work for but who also 'comes under' an office supervisor. They might not find it easy to tell you which is their 'real' boss.

Maybe you too have more than one person in your working life who can 'call the shots'. How many people are entitled to make demands on you? How many are capable of helping or hindering you in getting what you want out of your work? Maybe more than just the one you normally think of as 'the boss'.

Anyone who has this sort of power over you may be worth thinking of as a kind of boss. Even if you have one obvious boss, you may be able to think of certain other individuals, almost as powerful, whose good-will you need in getting what you want. Think, perhaps, of your boss's boss or of managers of other sections, or of specialists like accountants and personnel officers.

On the one hand, you may need to manage them in such a way as to get what you want from your boss – e.g. by winning their heavyweight backing for your ideas. On the other hand, you may need to manage your boss in such a way as to keep these other 'bossy' types off your back.

Anyway, the main point here is that, if you are to manage such people who can affect what you get out of your work, you will need to *know* them. The more you know about them, the more effectively you should be able to influence them – or resist their influence. If you have an obvious boss, he or she is the person it is most vital to know. But also learn what you can about any others who may make things better or worse for you.

MULTIPLE BOSSES

Multiple bosses can be both a blessing and a curse. On the plus side, you may be able to play one off against the other(s). At any particular moment, none of them is likely to have a very intimate knowledge of the priorities of the others. So you may have more room to decide your own priorities – regretfully telling Boss A that you can't tackle his or her project just yet because you're working on something very urgent for Boss B. Or, of course, you may, if you feel so inclined, offer to 'squeeze it in somehow' – *as a special favour*. Done skilfully, that should leave him or her feeling they owe you something!

On the negative side, however, multiple bosses can be a pain in the neck – and for exactly the same reason I mention above. None is properly aware of what the others are demanding of you. So they all demand too much, as if each of them were the only one you are working for.

They may not believe the 'I'm afraid I'm already piled up with work from Mrs X or Mr Y' excuse. If they don't, then you may need to find a way of getting them together to discuss your workload. Let them decide between them what their *combined* priorities are. Let them sort out which of them is going to get what proportion of your limited time and energies, and in what order. When they realize how much you are being put upon, they may even decide you need some extra resources!

WHAT IS A BOSS, ANYWAY?

Just what is a boss? Usually, we think of them as some sort of manager or supervisor. Neither of these terms need appear in the person's title, of course. They may be called Co-ordinator, Team Leader, Section Head, Executive Officer, Senior this or Chief that, or just Mrs Smith or Mr Jones, or Sue or Bob.

The main thing that distinguishes a boss from a non-boss is that bosses are responsible for other people's work. Their role, as the saying goes, is 'to achieve results through the efforts of other people'. You are one of those 'other people'. If you yourself have 'other people' to supervise, then you are a boss as well. (Nearly all bosses have bosses themselves. This can be a helpful point to remember if you are having trouble with your own boss.)

So what is a boss actually meant to do? What they are meant to do is manage.

IS YOUR BOSS REALLY MANAGING?

Managing involves:

- PLANNING the results to be obtained from other people's efforts;
- ORGANIZING those people and all appropriate resources to get the necessary work done; and
- MONITORING the outcomes of that work (day to day, week to week) with a view to
- CORRECTING deviations from the plan – or taking advantage of new opportunities to update it.

Does your boss spend most of his or time on these sorts of activities? They will involve him or her in a lot of talk – with you and your colleagues, with his or her boss, with other managers. There will be frequent meetings, discussions, and conversations.

Your boss will be making decisions on the basis of all this

talking. He or she will be discussing these decisions with you, or at least telling you what they are. He or she will be keeping an eye on how you are getting on with your part of the work. This 'eye' may be close and very frequent, especially if the work is new or difficult. But if the work is largely routine and your boss trusts you, he or she may check up on you less often.

Either way, your boss should ensure that you know what you are supposed to be doing and should be giving you regular 'feedback'. That is, she or he should be reassuring you that your work continues to be satisfactory – or, if not, discussing with you why it is not satisfactory and what can be done to improve it.

When Managers Aren't Managing

So those are the kinds of activity that bosses should spend most of their time on. Oddly enough, many don't. Many spend a lot of their time doing the same kinds of work they were doing *before* they got to be managers. For instance, they carry on selling, or designing or making things, rather than concentrating on *managing* the work of other people carrying out those tasks.

There are many reasons why this happens. After all, they probably got promoted because they were good at those tasks, and they don't want to lose their old skills. In fact, if they've had no training as managers, some may feel more comfortable with the old tasks than with the managerial duties that are now expected of them. Others may spend a lot of their time doing the job (*your* job, maybe) rather than managing it, for such reasons as the following:

- 'I want the team to know that I can do anything I ask them to do.'
- 'I can often do the work better than they can; and if you want a job doing really well, it's usually safer to do it yourself.'
- 'I like my staff to see that I haven't got too big-headed to turn my own hand to the work.'

It's true that many management jobs do involve the boss in doing some of the same work that is done by the people she or he is managing. Especially when there is a sudden pile-up of work or a flu epidemic hits the section.

But some bosses do too much – at the expense of their ability to manage. It can be very frustrating to have bosses who used to do your job. They may be forever nit-picking over the details of your work because they don't trust you to do it as well as they used to. This may be especially irritating if you feel they are not spending enough time looking after the work of the section as a whole – and are not giving you the kind of freedom and support you'd really find useful.

If you feel your boss is spending too much time on the wrong kind of activities, discuss it with your colleagues. You may want to give some thought to how you can encourage your boss to change his or her ways.

HOW DID YOUR BOSS GET TO BE BOSS?

If you are to influence your boss, it may help to know how she or he got to be boss. As I've suggested above, many 'come up through the ranks'. They weren't made boss because they showed 'managerial potential'. They got to be boss because they were outstandingly good at selling, accountancy, training, or whatever – so who better to put in charge of other sales staff, accountants, trainers, etc? (Some, perhaps, weren't even good at the job – just good at making an impression on their own boss!)

Unfortunately, there is no logical reason why the person who is good at doing a particular job should be good at managing the work of other people doing that job. Sometimes they are, of course. Indeed it can be positively helpful to be managed by someone who really understands your problems because they've been in your position themselves. Other 'players turned manager' can be a pain in the neck, however, as we've seen.

The Peter Principle

Some bosses just shouldn't be in their present jobs at all. They are living examples of 'The Peter Principle' – so named after the management writer who first drew it to the world's attention. The Peter Principle states that organizations tend to promote people to the level at which they become *incompetent*.

Such bosses are often aware, consciously or unconsciously, that they are out of their depth. But someone (their own boss, no doubt) made them an offer they felt they couldn't refuse. Promotion or dishonour! And now they live in fear of getting egg on their faces – and of being outflanked by any of their staff who've got more of what it takes than they have themselves.

If you have such a boss, he or she may need very careful handling. Make sure they clearly see you as an ally and supporter rather than as a potential threat. Incompetent or not, they can still do you a great deal of damage if they take against you. (And don't be misled by those who are inclined to bully and bluster. They may be the very ones who are most paranoid.)

YOUR LOCAL MANAGEMENT CULTURE

How good a manager your boss is likely to be may depend to a large extent on how the *profession* of management is viewed within your organization. And, of course, on how it is viewed by your manager in particular.

Consider factors like these:

- How much management experience has your boss had?
- Has your boss had experience of managing people doing work different from the sort she or he used to do?
- Has your boss had any training as a manager?
- Does she or he show any awareness of wanting to learn to be a better manager?

- Does the 'culture' within your organization encourage the idea of management as a profession that needs to be learned?

Is Your Boss a Thinking Manager?

Only a very small percentage of bosses have had any sort of training in management. Most are simply left to pick it up as they go along, learning from experience. Often this means they more or less copy their own boss's ways of doing things. They manage you as they themselves are managed – for better or worse.

Others, however, are more independent. Perhaps they have strong ideas of their own. Perhaps they are especially good at managing their boss (and thus winning space to do things their own way).

These may be the bosses who have realized early on that there *is* something to be learned about managing – and that it may not come from experience alone. Hence, they will talk to other managers about common problems. They will read books and articles about management. They are the ones who seem prepared to *think* about what managing involves.

Helping Your Boss to Develop

Is there any sign that your boss gives such thought to the art of management? If so, she or he may be easier to deal with. More reasonable, more open to alternatives perhaps.

If not, you and your colleagues may have to find your own ways of getting the boss to consider alternative ways of managing. For instance, browse along the overflowing shelves of management paperbacks in any large bookshop. Pick out a few titles like *The One-Minute Manager* or *How to be a Better Manager* or *The Manager's Book of Checklists*. If you like any of their ideas, try bringing them to your boss's attention.

You might find it productive to ask your boss's opinion or experience of certain management approaches you think may be relevant to work in your section – starting perhaps with approaches that are not too wildly different from the way your boss manages at the moment. You should know your boss well enough to decide whether and how best to raise such matters.

If you are a boss yourself, you'll maybe have more up-to-date ideas on management than your boss has. If you are not, then it's still quite possible that you'll have reflected enough on management – maybe you've experienced quite a variety of bosses – to know that your boss's way may not always be the only or best way. At all events, don't assume that your boss will *automatically* have a greater understanding of management than you have.

WHAT'S YOUR BOSS'S MANAGEMENT STYLE?

There are many different ways in which your boss might manage. Some of these might suit you more than others.

Some bosses just *tell* you what's to be done and how to do it. Some try to *sell* you what they've decided is best. Others *consult* you on what's to be done and get you to contribute to the decisions. Yet others may actually *delegate* at least some of the decision-making for you to take care of on your own.

Here are seven bosses talking about the approach they usually take. Which sounds most like your boss? Which approach would you prefer your boss to take?

A. 'I decide what to do and simply tell my staff to get
   on with it.'   [ ]
B. 'I decide what needs doing but then I explain to
   my staff why it needs to be done.'   [ ]
C. 'I decide what to do but I invite questions and
   comments from staff in case I see ways I can
   improve my decision.'   [ ]
D. 'I present staff with one or more tentative solutions
   to a problem and invite discussion of them before
   I make the final decision.'   [ ]

    E. 'I present staff with the problem and get them to
       come up with possible solutions before I make the
       decision.'   [ ]
    F. 'I present staff with the problem and let them
       make the decision.'   [ ]
    G. 'I expect staff to both define the problem and
       decide what to do about it (subject to certain
       limits).'   [ ]

If your boss is like those towards the bottom of the list, then
you will have more freedom and responsibility within your
work than if she or he is like those nearer the top of the
list.

Whether you are happy about your boss's approach is
another matter. You may feel your boss is too directive –
giving you little or no chance to influence important decisions. On the other hand, you may feel she or he spends
too much time consulting you and your colleagues. Perhaps
you'd just as soon be clearly told what needs to be done –
especially if the task is a fairly straightforward one or you
take the view that the boss is paid to take the tough decisions
so why should you help out!

Is Your Boss Consistent?
Perhaps the main thing you'll look for in your boss's approach
is *consistency*:

- Do you know what your boss's approach is likely to be –
  e.g. will he or she tell you what to do or ask your views –
  with the various kinds of problems that are likely to arise
  in your work together?
- Can you rely on your boss to consult you over things
  that really matter to you?
- Will he or she pay attention to what you have to say and
  let you contribute to the decision?
- Will your boss's boss support any decisions that you
  have contributed to?
- Does your boss have sufficient 'clout' within the organization to be able to manage as you'd prefer?

Many people don't mind too much what sort of bosses they have, so long as they know where they are with them. The sort they can't stand are those who are sometimes heavy-handed, sometimes very democratic – but with no apparent reason for the differences. Has their own manager started breathing down their necks? Have they just come back from the latest course? Have they got trouble at home?

Most of us want a boss whose approach we can predict, even if we don't always like it. And if our boss suddenly adopts an approach that seems untypical, it makes us uneasy, and we want to know why. (And the best way to find out, of course, is to ask – the approach may turn out not be as illogical as it looks.)

Remember that the boss's job is to get tasks performed by other people (like you). Some bosses concentrate on making the people happy at the expense of getting the tasks performed. Others concentrate on getting the tasks performed and neglect the welfare and needs of the people doing them.

Well-balanced Bossing
Does your boss fall into either of the above categories? Or does she or he get the balance just about right? Ask yourself which of the following your boss has done in managing your work over the last few weeks:

- Reminded you and your colleagues how the work of your section fits in with the work of the organization as a whole.   [ ]

- Brought you up to date on any changes within the organization that may affect the work of your section.   [ ]

- Shared with you any of his or her own thoughts and feelings about the future work of the section.   [ ]

- Invited you to contribute your thoughts and feelings about the work of the section, or about your own job.   [ ]

- Showed signs of having taken into account your
  viewpoints (and/or those of your colleagues)
  in making decisions about the work of the section.   [ ]

- Explained all decisions he or she has taken that
  affect your work.   [ ]

- Delegated decision-making where appropriate.   [ ]

- Said anything to you about the purpose/
  importance of your own job and how it contributes
  to the section.   [ ]

- Made clear exactly what is expected of you and
  explained any changes that have become necessary
  from time to time.   [ ]

- Given you praise (or criticism) about *specific*
  aspects of your work – not just generalized pats
  on the back or grumblings.   [ ]

- Supported you in getting what you want from
  your work and/or doing it better.   [ ]

- Encouraged you in gaining new expertise and/or
  becoming capable of more satisfying work.   [ ]

- Monitored the progress of your section's work
  and kept you and your colleagues informed as
  to how you and the section as a whole are
  progressing with that work.   [ ]

- Shown that he or she cares about you and your
  colleagues as individuals and recognizes that you
  have a life outside the organization – which may
  affect your life at work (and vice versa).   [ ]

- Been available, approachable and willing
  to listen to any matters of concern you wanted
  to raise.   [ ]

These fifteen items are just a few of the things you might expect from a good boss. No doubt you can think of several more. Many bosses would swear they do them all anyway – yet their staff will often tell you otherwise.

Which of the items do you most value? Personally, I most appreciate a boss:

(a) who lets me in on his or her thinking;

(b) who sets me clear goals – or, preferably, agrees such goals with me after hearing my views and taking them into account; and

(c) who gives me regular feedback about how he or she sees my work – and not just in such broad and unhelpful terms as 'You're doing a great job' or 'It's time you pulled your socks up', but by giving me constructive comments on specific weaknesses I can correct or strengths I can build upon.

Influencing Your Boss's Style

What if your boss doesn't give you the kind of management you want? Well, this is where you need to exercise *your* management skills – gently training your boss to give you what you need. Usually this means talking to your boss, presenting your views, asking for more information.

I wouldn't be satisfied, for example, with my boss saying: 'Your letter-writing just isn't good enough.' I would say something like: 'I'm glad you've told me. If we look at two or three of the letters I've written recently, perhaps you can show me where the main faults are and how I might improve them?'

With some bosses I've known I'd be inclined to put this response in writing. Why? Just in case they don't care to go into details with me because they don't quite see how to back up their original accusation, yet still might feel moved to badger me with it at a later date. If they know you can prove that you were ready and willing to do something about an alleged fault, yet they weren't, they may feel less eager to mention it again.

IS YOUR BOSS HUMAN?

Many people have such a ground-in respect for authority-figures that they forget their boss is human like the rest of us. They therefore regard them as a different form of life – creatures who couldn't possibly have the same sort of concerns as those we chat to quite naturally in a pub or in the supermarket queue.

As a result, they never dream of approaching the boss themselves but always wait to be summoned. And, if summoned, they go along fearful of what the boss might have to tell them – rather than pleased to have the opportunity to make a few points of their own.

Dealing With Authority

To some extent, we are all victims of our upbringing. Parents, teachers, doctors, politicians, religious leaders, and other people have been telling us what's good for us from our earliest years. Some of us never quite free ourselves of the feeling that such authority-figures are more likely to be right than we are.

Others vehemently reject them as soon as they feel big enough and strong enough. They refuse to accept that anything an authority-figure says can ever be believed – 'Don't trust anybody over thirty.' Some women, especially in male-dominated organizations, have learned to say 'Don't trust men.'

Yet other people are prepared to judge authority-figures on their merits (or lack of them). They see that individuals differ. One boss, for example, may be more worth listening to than others. Indeed the same boss may be very sound in some areas, less so in others. What kind of attention you pay to your authority-figures must depend on what you know of their personal strengths and weaknesses.

Bosses, like other authority-figures, are individuals. Certainly they are different from the rest of us – but only because they have more *power*. How they exercise that power (and how we can influence it) depends to a very large extent on what they are like as human beings.

If you have a remote and arrogant boss, it may be difficult to think of him or her as a human being. One woman told me she'd found it impossible to talk naturally to her rather pompous soberly-suited boss until the image had suddenly entered her head of him sitting on the lavatory with his pin-striped trousers round his ankles.

What's Your Boss Like?

Anyway, it's as well to find out all you can about your boss as a human being. For instance:

- What are your boss's likes and dislikes?
- What are his or her hobby-horses?
- Is he or she married, with or without children?
- What are his or her political/religious affiliations?
- Which newspaper does he or she read?
- What clubs, activities, and outside interests is your boss involved with? (Can you honestly share an interest in any of these?)
- Do you and your boss have a similar sense of humour?
- How tolerant is your boss of people who are different from him or her?
- How is your boss's work affected by family and/or social life outside the organization?
- How is he or she regarded by other people?
- How would he or she like to be regarded?
- What is he or she looking for from life and from work? (How might this compare with your own answers to this question in Chapter 1?)
- What personal ambitions does your boss have?
- What, if anything, does he or she fear or have anxieties about?
- What is he or she looking for from you?

What Can You Offer?

If you are to manage your boss, you need to know him or her as a human being. You won't get anything of value from your boss unless you offer something he or she values in exchange. So you need to know what it is he or she values.

What is your boss most anxious to attain – or most anxious to avoid? Is he or she obsessed with reaching higher and higher rank in the organization? Or is he or she more preoccupied with avoiding being unmasked as a bit of a wimp? Or is he or she concerned only to make your section as congenial and productive as the best in your organization?

Once you know what makes him or her tick, you can look for ways to:

1. Convince your boss that he or she can rely on you to help him or her achieve what he or she wants to achieve – or avoid what he or she fears.
2. Enable your boss to realize just how dependent he or she is on your continuing support.
3. Graciously accept the benefits that your boss is persuaded to grant you in order to ensure your support does continue.

Trading Favours

If this sounds a bit like blackmail, it shouldn't. For one thing, it is mutual. You will be equally dependent on your boss and on his or her continuing support in getting what you want out of work. You are both in the same boat.

The main difference is that you will be ensuring that your boss is just as aware of the dependency as you are. Normally, only the managed feel dependent. They don't bring home to the boss how impotent and exposed he or she will be without their support.

Besides, mutual dependency and the trading of favours is just the everyday stuff of human contact. If, for example, we stop giving our friends the kind of support they've come to expect from us, they eventually cease to find us attractive as friends. They may say 'we seem to have grown apart'. Mutual support is what friendship is all about and whether or not he or she thinks of you as a friend, your boss needs to see that he or she must give you what you want in return for what he or she wants.

HOW TO FIND OUT ABOUT THE BOSS

As I've suggested several times, the more you know about your boss, the better the position you'll be in – both to offer your boss appropriate support and to persuade your boss to support you. So how do you get the information you need?

What Your Boss Tells You
Your most important source is the boss himself or herself. Talk as much as possible with your boss – or rather get your boss talking and do plenty of listening.

Listen not just for what he or she says but also for the way it is said. Which subjects does your boss speak of with confidence and optimism; and which with anxiety or alarm? And what is left unsaid? Are there any subjects your boss seems unwilling to talk about at all?

Look out too for the 'body language' – those bodily movements that indicate when a person is feeling enthusiastic and alert or, let's say, anxious and ill at ease.

Every encounter with your boss should tell you more about her or him. The kinds of situation where you are putting a proposal to your boss, or trying to win her or him over to your point of view (see Chapter 7), should be particularly revealing. So too should situations like an appraisal interview (see Chapter 8). But even the briefest of conversations may give you insights you'll be able to use in your future dealings with your boss.

After each encounter with your boss, ask yourself: 'What have I learned about my boss (and perhaps about myself) that might help me in my future forays into boss-management?'

What Your Colleagues Can Tell You

All the colleagues in your section should be a useful source of knowledge about your boss. Together you should have a pool of experience you can all draw upon.

Different people will have different kinds of dealings with the boss, of course. They may therefore have formed quite different impressions – perhaps because they act (and are reacted to) quite differently from you. So take what you hear from other people with a pinch of salt. Ask yourself how much it is telling you about the boss rather than about the person whose story you are hearing.

Do make a friend of your boss's secretary or closest assistants. They can give you a lot of useful information, without being in the least disloyal, simply by the way they speak about the boss. They may also be able to help you get access to him or her, and may even advise you on how best to present your proposals.

Other Sources

Don't neglect the wider information networks. People in other sections, your boss's boss, other clients and customers, and so on. They may all offer you new and useful slants on your boss's little ways. Even if they don't always put their reactions into words, you may still learn quite a bit about your boss from the way those other people appear to act towards him or her. Keep your eyes and ears open!

I do not recommend organizational espionage as a means of finding out about the boss – however popular it may be in some quarters. I remember one colleague in an organization I once worked for whose rapid promotion was widely understood to be due to his outstanding appetite for hard work – evidenced by the fact that he was still in the office many hours after everyone else had gone home.

It was only after he was ignominiously 'let go' that the news got around that his staying on late certainly had played a part in his brief run of success – but only because it gave him the opportunity to analyse the contents of his boss's wastepaper bin and, eventually, to penetrate the filing cabinets holding his personal correspondence and details about other staff. That character ended up knowing far more about his boss (and others) than anyone could legitimately be expected to know – but lacked the wit to conceal it!

Chapter 4

Know Your Job

One of the key elements in managing your boss is getting his or her agreement as to what your job is. Surprisingly, many people, some of them bosses themselves, seem incapable of saying exactly what they are supposed to be doing.

There are a few who are quite happy with this state of affairs – 'If it's not clear what I'm responsible for, then I can't be blamed if things go wrong.'

But they may be living in cloud-cuckoo-land. It's just as likely they can be blamed for *anything* that goes wrong if they can't prove it wasn't part of their job. It's no defence to say 'Nobody ever told me I was expected to see to that.'

Besides, to look at the other side of the coin, they can't claim credit for doing things well if their boss never agreed what things they should be doing.

SOME BASIC QUESTIONS

Here are some basic questions about your job:

- Does it have a title that indicates how it relates to other people's jobs?   [ ]
- Can you state the overall *purpose* of your job in a single sentence?   [ ]
- Can you explain how your work connects up with that of other people in the section and the organization?   [ ]

- Can you list your main duties and
  responsibilities?   [ ]
- Can you list any objectives or targets you are
  expected to achieve?   [ ]
- Can you say what your boss will be looking for
  in judging your performance at work?   [ ]
- Are you confident that your boss would agree
  with how you have answered the above questions?   [ ]

Your progress at work will be judged on your performance. And your performance will be judged against certain criteria. It's not good enough that your boss should know what those criteria are. You, too, need to know (and preferably have some say in) what those criteria are to be. You need a written *job description* and/or *work plan*.

WHAT MAKES A GOOD JOB DESCRIPTION?

A worthwhile job description should be a statement of what you are supposed to DOING and ACHIEVING, and of what your responsibilities are. It should cover at least three aspects:

1. Your main duties.
2. Any specific targets or objectives that you are expected to achieve.
3. Any responsibility you may have for staff or resources.

Staff and Resources
Let's look at the third item first:
- Are you responsible for the work of any other
  staff? (That is, are you a boss yourself?)   [ ]
- Are you responsible for spending any of your
  section's money? (For example, can you approve
  purchases?)   [ ]
- Are you responsible for approving the use of
  valuable equipment or facilities, or for ensuring
  they are properly looked after?   [ ]

If your answer to any of the above questions is YES, then the *limits* of your responsibility should be made clear in your job description. *Which* staff are you responsible for? *How much* expenditure can you approve without checking with your boss? What exactly is the *nature* of your responsibility for *which* equipment and facilities?

If none of these items appear in your job description, it might be as well to check that they're not meant to. As one secretary told me only a few days ago: 'I'd been wondering for ages why people kept coming to me about problems with the photocopiers.' Other people had been told that she was responsible for these machines, but her boss had omitted to tell her.

Main Duties and Objectives

Now let's consider items 1 and 2. 'Main duties' are the *activities* on which you will be spending your time at work. They cover the things you will be doing – whether every day or just now and again. (If you happen to be a boss yourself, they may include the things you are responsible for getting other people to do.)

The second item, however, is concerned with the *results* of these activities. Objectives or targets are what you will reach or achieve as a result of carrying out one or more of your main duties. This may mean getting certain production projects completed by a certain date, for example, or reducing the rejects within a certain clerical process to an acceptable, agreed percentage.

Here are some examples, each from a different person's job description:

Some main duties
- Collect and deliver internal mail
- Prepare specimens for microscopic analysis
- Record and safeguard prisoners' property
- Maintain cash books, day journals and ledgers
- Ensure building work is carried out according to specification

Some targets/objectives
- Get all new staff trained by end of November
- Reduce the section's non-staff costs by at least 10% by the end of the year
- Ensure publication of audit by June 1st
- Reach at least 50 words per minute on in-house typing course
- Ensure each client has been visited at least four times in the year

Your main duties may remain pretty similar from year to year. They probably won't be exactly the same, though. Jobs do change and job descriptions easily get out of date if they are not looked at regularly.

Targets and objectives, however, are more likely to vary from year to year. In fact your boss may want you to change them, or take on new ones, at any time. If so, it is important that you agree whether such new targets or objectives are really practicable. And at what cost – e.g. what extra resources will need to be provided or what other targets will have to be given a lower priority?

Not all jobs lend themselves to the setting of targets or objectives – except perhaps as a matter of daily or weekly routine (e.g. the pay packets must be got ready every Friday by 4pm).

But where targets or objectives can be set, they give you a date to aim at and/or a level or result to be attained. How would you regard this:

  a) as a burden or even a threat? [ ]
or b) as a challenge or a way of *proving* to your
     boss that you are working effectively? [ ]

Presumably your answer will depend on how far your boss has taken your views into consideration in setting the objectives. And on whether you think they are fair and attainable.

SORTING THINGS OUT WITH YOUR BOSS

So you need a written statement of what you are supposed to be doing and achieving and what you are responsible for. In your organization you may find such documents called job descriptions, work plans, or something else together.

You may find they are revised annually, or more frequently, or not at all. You may find you are expected to write or update your own, to take whatever your boss hands out, or to agree it in discussion.

Or, of course, you may find that such documents just don't seem to exist in your organization.

Whatever the situation, a vital part of managing your boss consists of getting a piece of paper that sets out the kind of information we have been discussing above. Otherwise, you won't be able to demonstrate to your boss that you have been doing the job, the whole job and (if they're that kind of boss) nothing but the job.

Common Problems

Whether you are drafting your own job description or 'agreeing' one provided by your boss, there are certain problems to look out for. Most of them are listed below – together with my comments and suggested solutions:

1. Are any of your duties described in such vague or general terms that you and your boss might disagree as to what you are supposed to be doing? For instance, 'organize meetings' might mean that you are expected to confirm people's availability, decide on best timing, book a suitable room, circulate necessary papers – or it might mean just some (or none) of these activities and/or several more besides.

   If so, aim to get such duties spelled out in terms of the specific activities.

2. Is it clear which duties will occupy most time and which least? For instance, two people could each have

the same two duties (Duty X and Duty Y) and yet be doing two very different jobs. How so? Because one person is expected to spend 90% of their time on Duty X while the other person is expected to spend 90% of their time on Duty Y.

If possible, rank your duties in order, from those taking up most to those taking up least time. And try to state the approximate percentage of your total time that each will occupy.

3. Can you tell the difference between the most time-consuming duties and the most critical ones? For instance, a duty carried out briefly once a month or even once a year could involve your organization in huge embarrassment or financial loss, or could be dangerous to your health, if you did it less than well.

   Add a note to your job description to highlight such potentially costly or hazardous duties.

4. Are all the duties listed really *yours*? 'Spare' duties sometimes creep into a job description merely because they sound like others on the list – or perhaps because old Chris, who did the job last year, just happened to fancy doing them.

   Delete any duties you believe you shouldn't be doing – and would not want your boss to judge you by.

5. Have any important duties been omitted? If your job is changing, a job description will soon get out of date and need amending. Look also for extra duties that would make your job more of a satisfying 'whole' and enable you to get more of what you want out of work.

   Add any missing duties or desirable duties and be prepared to convince your boss that you should take on the latter. This may be easier if you can show that they are important and that no one else will be doing them if you don't.

6. Have all foreseeable objectives, targets, deadlines, results, etc, been mentioned? Don't allow your boss to

clobber you later on with some such line as 'If you didn't realize that survey was to be completed by the end of June you should have told me.'

Ask your boss if there are any objectives etc. she or he has omitted to mention. Make it clear that you are not aware of, and are not working towards, any that are not explicitly stated.

7. Are all objectives etc. precise enough that you can be sure exactly what you need to do to satisfy your boss? Objectives may be vague or not specific enough – e.g. 'Improve time-keeping' or 'Cut down on waste'. What might the boss regard as a satisfactory improvement or cutting down?

Re-write vague objectives so that there can be no doubt as to whether they have been attained – e.g. 'Don't be late by more than a total of 15 minutes in any week' and 'Reduce waste by 20% by the end of the month'.

8. Are the proposed objectives etc. realistic and attainable? Don't agree to pursue the impossible dream – e.g. 'Never be late again' or 'End waste completely as of now'.

Modify any obviously unattainable objectives.

9. Have the nature and limits of your responsibility for staff and other resources been clearly stated? Unless they have, you run the risk of being unfairly accused of having exceeded your authority – or of not having exercised it.

Make sure that your job description or work plan lists any staff you are responsible for, and what aspects of their work. (Maybe you'll need to discuss *their* job descriptions.) The extent or circumstances in which you are expected/allowed to make decisions, change priorities, authorize expenditure etc, may also need to be spelled out.

While you are discussing your job with your boss, here is a final question to consider:

HOW MIGHT YOUR JOB BE IMPROVED?

One thing you might want from your boss is to get your present job improved. (You may also want to get promoted to a different job, but that's another matter.) Is there anything your boss might do to help make your present work more satisfying?

For example, might you welcome improvement along any of these lines:

- Making the job more of a *whole* – so that it makes more of an identifiable contribution to the team's and/or organization's eventual product or service? [ ]

- Adding elements to it that make it seem more meaningful and worth doing? (For example, giving you more contact with users of the product or service you are contributing to.) [ ]

- Making greater call on your skills and experience – or perhaps drawing on skills that have so far gone unused (e.g. in training new colleagues)? [ ]

- Offering more scope for learning and personal development (perhaps with a view to promotability)? [ ]

- Giving you a greater variety of tasks or types of activity? [ ]

- Allowing you more freedom to make decisions in doing your work? [ ]

- Giving you more frequent feedback about the effectiveness of your performance? [ ]

- Making the job more demanding or challenging?   [ ]

- Allowing more satisfactory contact with
  colleagues – e.g. in team projects?   [ ]

- Others (what?)   . . .

If you feel your job might be improved – not just for your benefit but for that of your section – consider discussing it with your boss.

Your boss may or may not know of three 'standard' approaches to improving jobs. These are known as Job Rotation, Job Enlargement, and Job Enrichment. Consider whether you might benefit from any of them:

Job Rotation
You and your colleagues would 'rotate' from one job to another within the team – perhaps every few hours, days or weeks, according to the sort of work you do. This might provide a more satisfying variety of work and help you all develop new skills.

Some people might not like it, of course, preferring the settled routine of a job they are thoroughly familiar with. And your boss might feel it would make uncomfortable demands on his or her ability to organize the rota and provide any necessary training or support in the early stages.

Job Enlargement
Here you would carry out a 'cluster' of related tasks rather than just one of them. For example, suppose there are four stages in assembling a machine (or processing a customer's order) and that you and three colleagues are each responsible for one of them. Instead, you might each carry out all four stages – so that each of you would assemble a complete machine (or completely process an order) rather than do just part of the job.

This might make the work seem more meaningful, more of a 'whole'. On the other hand, you and/or some of your colleagues might be happier to stick with your own specialist responsibility. Again, your boss might be concerned about having to provide new training for each of you. On the other hand, she or he might see the advantage in having each of you capable of doing the whole job – especially if one of you were suddenly to go sick or leave the section.

Job Enrichment

Here your boss would need to enable you to extend your job by, e.g.:

- taking more responsibility for deciding your own objectives and/or ways of working;
- using feedback to monitor your own performance;
- undertaking additional tasks that were not previously done by someone of your 'grade'; and
- acquiring and using new skills and expertise.

This approach is sometimes used with a *group* of colleagues rather than with an individual. In other words, the group is given more responsibility for planning, organizing and monitoring the work of that group themselves – with less frequent or heavy direction than previously from a supervisor or manager.

What Suits Whom?

As always, such 'enrichment' may or may not fit in with what you want out of your work. Some people relish the opportunity to make their own decisions. Others prefer to settle for limited responsibility and not having to think too much about what they are doing. There's no right way to be. We are all different, and which way we are depends, very often, on the particular situation.

Where job enrichment is being tried with a working group, for instance, some colleagues may welcome the opportunity to work more closely with each other, while others may not – especially if interpersonal conflicts begin to emerge.

Again, your boss may or may not be easily persuaded that job enrichment would be good for the section as a whole (and therefore good for him or her). As with anything you want from your boss, it would be up to you to make out the best possible case for what you want. And the best possible case is one that makes clear *what's in it for him or her*. Though you might also need to spell out the benefits to the section and to the organization as a whole – just in case your boss has to 'sell on' your suggestion to his or her boss.

CONCLUSIONS

Ideally, you should be able to answer YES to the following questions:

- In general, am I sure that my boss and I are agreed about what I should be doing, what authority I have, and what results I will be judged by?   [ ]
- Am I satisfied that my boss's expectations are reasonable and realistic?   [ ]
- Do I feel that, at least for the present, the job is sufficiently 'stretching'?   [ ]

If you've answered NO to any of the above questions (or weren't sure what to answer), you may have problems doing your present job successfully. Either you aren't entirely satisfied with your job or you aren't as clear as you should be about what is expected of you.

Talk it over with your boss. If you haven't got a job description (or it's out of date), draw one up (or revise the old one). Let your boss know:

- what you believe to be the activities you are expected to be engaged in;
- the results you are expected to produce; and
- the authority you are expected to exercise.

And seek your boss's *agreement* so that – later on – you should both be able to agree whether you have done the job successfully. Remember that your work performance will be appraised on the basis of the job description you agree with your boss. So make sure that you and your boss have the SAME understanding of what you are supposed to be doing and achieving.

*   *   *

There are three key priorities in managing your boss, and in this chapter we have dealt with the first of them:
1. Know what your job IS.
   We'll go on to Points 2 and 3 in the next two chapters.
2. Do it SUCCESSFULLY.
3. Be SEEN to be doing it successfully.

Chapter 5

Do Your Job Well – and Visibly Well

Chapter 4 was about getting agreement as to what the boss expects of you in your job. This chapter is about providing it – AND about leaving the boss in no doubt that you are providing it. It's not enough to do the job well. You must be *seen* to do it well.

In some organizations, or with some bosses, cynics might (rightly) convert this too: 'It's not necessary to do the job well, so long as you *seem* to do it well.'

What we are talking about here is managing your boss's impression of your work. What kind of impression does your boss have of your work at present? Some people have told me that their bosses have no particular impression. Their work is just taken for granted. Or perhaps the individual's contribution is lost on the boss because he or she has a big team to manage.

This impression management is clearly important if you want to win any favours from your boss – a rise, some improvement of your job, a promotion. Your boss needs a clear and favourable impression of your work. Only then will she or he feel that giving you the 'reward' you seek may spur you to even better work – and yet more valuable support for the boss – in the future.

So how do you manage your boss's impression of your work? Here are some fairly basic suggestions:

STICK TO THE JOB

Make sure you are doing your job as you agreed it with your boss. You should have *your own copy* of the job description. Keep it somewhere where you can't help but see it from time to time. Make a point of checking through it regularly. Ask yourself:

- Am I carrying out *all* my duties – including the ones I am required to do only occasionally?
- Am I meeting any targets or objectives that were set?
- Am I exercising (but not exceeding) any responsibility I may have for people and resources?

Sticking to the job you're supposed to be doing means that you should avoid getting side-tracked into duties that are not in your job description. Suppose you found you were regularly being asked to carry out duties or aim for objectives that were not part of your job description or agreed work-plan. Here is how I've known various different people respond to this situation. Which of them would seem most appropriate in *your* situation?

- Accept it as part of the give-and-take of life in any working organization.
- Reject all such work as being none of your concern.
- Discuss with your boss whether your job description needs changing.
- Write the extra duties into your own copy of the job description, and get on with them.

BUT KEEP FLEXIBLE

No doubt it all depends how heavy and acceptable the new work is – and on who is asking you to do it. You probably can't just reject all extra duties or new objectives – especially when it's your boss who's asking. They may have become vital to the success of your section's work, because circumstances have changed since you agreed your work with the boss. But nor can you afford just to take them on without comment, even if you alter your own copy of the job description.

Doing extra duties, or tackling new objectives, may leave you with less time to do your agreed duties as well as you might have done. Thus, at appraisal time, you might get no credit for the extra work you did (maybe several months ago) because it was not mentioned in your job description – or, at least, not in your boss's copy.

Don't just rely on your boss's memory. By the end of the year you may not even have the same boss.

Rewrite Your Job Description?
If you are asked to tackle new duties or objectives, discuss with your boss the possible need to get them written into your 'official' job description or work plan. Similarly, if you are asked to give up certain duties or modify certain objectives, get it in writing.

Make sure that your job description or work plan CONTINUES to fit the job that your boss believes you to be doing.

What if you've got the sort of boss who wouldn't be bothered with such paperwork? Then do it yourself. Send him or her a dated note or a memo, setting out what you believe you have now been asked to do or achieve. Keep a copy for yourself.

GO FOR IT

Cultivate a 'go for it' attitude. Make sure you give the boss what he or she is expecting from your work – while at the same time getting what you want from it. Which of the following suggestions seem particularly relevant in your situation?

- Set yourself high standards.   [ ]

- Push yourself to improve on your past
  performance.   [ ]
- Don't waste time on inessentials.   [ ]
- Shrug off failures, and go all the harder for
  your next objective.   [ ]
- Respond constructively to constructive criticism.   [ ]
- Think positively about the future, rather
  than negatively about the past. Don't say
  'If only I'd done such-and-such' but tell
  yourself *'Next time*, I will do such-and-such.'   [ ]
- Keep your eyes open for new opportunities.   [ ]
- Look for ways of improving things.   [ ]
- Be enthusiastic, and encourage enthusiasm
  in those around you.   [ ]
- Be courageous and take calculated risks.   [ ]
- Work hard to get *results* (not just to
  fulfil duties).   [ ]
- But don't alienate your colleagues by
  flaunting your prodigious work-rate.   [ ]
- Others (what?)   . . .

MONITOR YOUR OWN WORK

Your boss may or may not be keeping a regular eye on your work. He or she may be giving you frequent or occasional feedback – and may or may not be sizing you up towards some sort of end-of-year 'appraisal'. Either way, you should be constantly appraising your own work – both your strengths and your weaknesses.

Remedy Your Shortcomings
Ideally, you should always be one step ahead of the boss. You will normally know how things are going sooner than he or she will. You should be in a position to spot your

own shortcomings – and perhaps to do whatever is needed to remedy them – before your boss has even noticed them. Sometimes, however, this will not be possible.

Suppose you realize you simply *cannot* meet certain objectives, or perform certain duties to the standard expected of you. Which of the following common approaches do you think would go down best with *your* boss?

- Do as well as I can and hope that things
  miraculously work out. [ ]
- Keep going and hope the boss doesn't notice. [ ]
- Wait till the boss notices, but have my
  excuses ready. [ ]
- Explain the problem to the boss before
  he/she notices. [ ]
- Bring it to the boss's attention and ask him
  or her to sort it out. [ ]

Whatever kind of boss you've got, the best approach is unlikely to be sticking your head in the sand. You'll probably be betting on a loser if you think your shortcomings won't be noticed or will sort themselves out if left alone.

Nor can everyone's boss be satisfied with excuses. Even explanations may come too late to satisfy if you've left it to the boss to point out your shortcomings.

Most people will find that explaining the problem to the boss *before* she or he notices will be the most productive approach. It shows that you are conscious of the standards you should be working to and that you are concerned if you seem likely to fall short.

But do try to present your boss with some possible solutions, rather than just a problem. Give some thought to one or two possible remedies – e.g. temporary extra staff, more training, a longer deadline – rather than simply leaving it to your boss to sort it out for you. That way you'll get credit for being creative, rather than being blamed as the bringer of bad news.

Claim Your Successes

Most of the time, however, we must except that things will be going well in the job. You'll be satisfied with your performance and results – even delighted about one or two special successes or improvements.

You may hope that your boss will have noticed, and will be in agreement with your own self-appraisal. He or she may make this obvious with the occasional pat on the back or encouraging remark.

If you get such feedback, don't let yourself be overcome with false modesty. Good work deserves a good response. If you even suggest that 'There was nothing to it' or 'Anyone could have done it' or 'It's all part of the job', then your boss may begin to doubt his or her judgement – and be less likely to praise such a performance another time.

Some bosses are not too observant, however. You may need to bring some of your triumphs to your boss's attention. If necessary, don't hesitate to let him or her know when you are particularly pleased with a piece of work.

Do so without seeming to be fishing for compliments, of course. Rather than saying 'Didn't I do that job well?' say 'I'm very pleased with the way that job went'. But make sure your boss realizes that you are the one responsible for making it go well.

KEEP A WORK DIARY

Your boss may be keeping notes about your performance (and that of your colleagues). This is particularly likely if your organization, like so many nowadays, has a formal staff appraisal system. Your boss will then be keeping notes to aid his or her memory when it comes to writing your appraisal report at the end of the year. Clearly, your boss's notes will cover such issues as:

- how you have performed your main duties;
- the extent to which you have met targets or objectives;

- how well you have managed any staff or resources you are responsible for;
- any problems or difficulties your work has raised;
- any special performances that might support your promotability; and so on.

You need to ensure that you are in as good a position as your boss to look back over your performance at the end of the year. Thus you may want to keep notes – a 'paper memory' – of your own. Think of it as a Work Diary.

Is it Worthwhile?

Can this be worth the trouble, you may wonder. Well, I remember one boss, for example, who was planning to include 'poor time-keeping' on a person's end-of-year report because she had been late three times in the previous fortnight – which was about as far back as his unassisted memory could stretch. But this person had kept her own record of her time-keeping and was able to show that she had been late only six times in the previous eleven months, had always made up the lost time by working late, and had never previously been criticized by the boss.

It is worth keeping a notebook (not necessarily a Filofax!) in which to record such details, and your own notes on such items as those listed above. You may note the dates when certain projects were completed; jot down what your boss or other managers said to you on certain occasions; record examples of your having obviously improved at certain aspects of your work that may have been criticized in the past; and so on.

You can then refer to these notes if you do have an annual appraisal interview with your boss, or any other similar sort of discussion. They will be helpful if there is a difference of opinion – or if your boss's notes are rather less helpful to your case than your own are.

What's Worth Noting?

You will see below a fuller list of items you might want to

make notes on in a Work Diary. Which of them might you have written something about if you had been keeping such a diary over the last twelve months?

- The dates when projects were started and
  completed. [ ]
- The dates when targets/deadlines/objectives
  were reached. [ ]
- Tasks you did particularly well. [ ]
- Abilities you believe you have clearly
  improved in. [ ]
- Things you did less well than you
  (or your boss) would have liked. [ ]
- Praise or criticism from your boss or from
  other managers, clients, customers, etc. (Keep copies
  of any complimentary letters, memos, etc.) [ ]
- Training or extra help you've had from your boss or
  others, and what results it has had on your work. [ ]
- Training or extra help that was promised
  (perhaps at your last appraisal) but has not
  been provided. [ ]
- Unexpected problems that prevented you from
  doing as well as you expected to, e.g.:
  - illness [ ]
  - staff shortages [ ]
  - sudden rushes [ ]
  - extreme pressure [ ]
  - changes of deadlines [ ]
  - shortages of money and materials [ ]
  - problems with colleagues [ ]
  - problems with clients/customers [ ]
  - changes of duties [ ]
  - new objectives/targets/deadlines, etc. [ ]
  - others (what?)...
  (Be as specific as possible in recording such problems.)

The overall object of this exercise is to make sure that your memory of your work – and the success with which you are doing your job – is at least as sound (and preferably sounder) as that of your boss. This may be vital if you have an annual performance appraisal.

You must decide for yourself whether such a Work Diary might be worthwhile for you. The object would not be to make a daily chore of it or to produce your blow-by-blow memoirs of life at work. It would simply be to ensure that you have a written record of everything that might work to your advantage (or disadvantage) in any appraisals by your boss. A well-kept Work Diary can be a great comforter when the chips are down.

TALKING WITH YOUR BOSS

Try to talk regularly with your boss about how your work is going. Let your boss know that you are keeping your own Work Diary. Make sure he or she noticed your successes and the areas of work in which you have improved.

Be ready also to talk about your problems and difficulties as they arise. Maybe your boss has access to resources that can help overcome them. It will probably be better for you, and for the section, to tackle them early, before they get out of hand. Regard them as challenges to be met rather than as ace-up-your-sleeve excuses you'll be able to trot out later in the year if your performance turns out to have been not quite as healthy as expected.

Finally, you may think it wise to ask your boss for an informal appraisal of your work from time to time. You may want to ask how he or she thinks you are doing on one or more of your main duties. Perhaps you'll ask for an assessment on any aspect of your work that he or she has expressed concern about in the past. If your boss thinks you are still not up to scratch in some areas, you may then ask for help and advice to make any necessary improvements.

You may also want to record any criticisms and advice in your Work Diary. Clearly, you'd be wise to act on them and take up any special training or coaching that your boss is able to offer you. Make sure your boss knows that you are doing this. It would be very unreasonable of your boss to be highly critical later on – say in an end-of-year appraisal – if you have clearly invited criticism, and clearly acted upon it, throughout the year.

BE SEEN TO DO YOUR JOB SUCCESSFULLY

It is not enough to know your job and do it well. You must also be *seen* to do it well. VISIBILITY is the name of the game. This doesn't mean you have to go around shooting your mouth off about how brilliant you are. But it does mean you must not be reticent. Don't assume that such virtue as yours simply cannot go unnoticed and unrewarded. It can and it will, unless you bring it to people's attention.

The Finer Points of Impression Management
Here are a few suggestions, some of them recapping on points I have made above. Which of them seem applicable to your situation?

- Be open and confident about your work in talking to other people around the organization.
- However you present yourself, and whatever you say to your boss and other people around the organization, remember that folks are usually pretty willing to believe we are what we tell them we are – provided there is no blatant evidence to the contrary. Don't be unduly modest and certainly don't run yourself down.
- Don't be afraid to ask for help or advice from your colleagues. But ask for it as one who expects to be able to help them equally on other occasions. Don't pose as a know-it-all, but don't imply that you are basically incompetent, either. (I've heard not a few women apologetically muttering 'Of course, I'm just hopeless with

machines.' And I've heard as many men, rather more defiantly, saying 'I don't pretend to be able to deal with people's emotional problems.')

- Keep your boss up to date on your work progress, whether or not she or he has asked for a report. If she or he has asked for a progress report, attend to it without delay.
- Send your boss a brief note recording the completion of all major projects or objectives.
- Make sure he or she has noticed your successes and improvements. This applies especially to women, for women are generally more hesitant than men about drawing attention to their achievements.
- Ask your boss for an opinion as to how you are doing on some of your main duties – especially ones that have been criticized in the past and in which you know you have now improved.
- Point out the extra training, new methods, or other steps you have taken to improve your performance.
- Never express doubts as to your ability to quickly *acquire* whatever abilities are needed, even if you must admit that you don't have them all just yet.
- Don't moan to your boss about difficulties you are facing or blame your shortcomings on other people. Seek your boss's help in implementing possible solutions you have thought up, rather than in worrying about problems you've laid on his or her desk.
- Modestly pass onto your boss any praise you receive from elsewhere in the organization or from outside. This is likely to be especially helpful if your boss can interpret it as reflecting well on the section as a whole – and on him or her as the person responsible for your work. A copy of any congratulatory memo or letter – with a 'Thought you might be pleased to see this' written across the top – might be a useful way of letting your boss know how well-regarded you are.
- Cultivate what we might call 'champions' or 'sponsors' around the organization. These are people whom your

boss respects, for whom or with whom you have done good work, and who are prepared to speak well of you in public.

- If you are looking to earn promotion, remind your boss of this on every suitable occasion. Women, in particular, are often passed over for promotion because they have not made their ambitions clear. Members of ethnic minorities may also suffer from a similar invisibility. Remember: It's the squeaky wheel that gets the grease.

- Develop your skills. Don't ever let it be thought that you are complacent about your talents. Make it known that you believe in constant self-development and are always ready to learn. With some bosses, you may have to play this one carefully. They may think you are trying to self-develop yourself into their jobs – which is OK so long as they are confident about their own ability to self-develop themselves into even better ones.

This last point – about dedicating yourself to improve your competence – is such a powerful aid in both being and seeming successful that it's worth devoting the final section of this chapter to.

IMPROVE YOURSELF

I don't know what skills and competences are important in your work. I certainly don't know what skills and competences you might most usefully try to improve. All I can do is encourage you to give some serious thought to the matter and decide for yourself.

Obviously, there will be some abilities that are very specific to your particular job or organization. For example, you will need to be able to handle certain kinds of paperwork, or equipment or customer problems. Any weaknesses you have in such specific abilities should be pretty obvious to you. It may also be pretty obvious what you have to do to improve at them.

Some General Competences

However, there may also be some other types of more general ability or competence that are just as necessary. Indeed, they may be even more necessary if you want to be really successful at your job rather than just acceptably proficient.

I have listed a dozen such general competences below. Consider each one, decide whether it is especially relevant in doing well in your line of work, and tick it if it is one you feel you need to improve in:

- *Technical/professional knowledge*. How up-to-date are you in your knowledge of the product or service your organization (or section) provides?   [ ]
- *Organizational know-how*. How clued up are you about your organization's policies, plans, priorities, personalities, power struggles, politics, problems and outside reputation?   [ ]
- *Ability to grasp a situation*. How quick are you at sizing up a new situation, separating the relevant from the irrelevant in a new situation and seeing through to the key issues?   [ ]
- *Decision-making ability*. How confident are you of your ability to analyse the key issues in situations and make appropriate decisions fast enough?   [ ]
- *Creativity*. Are you able to come up with original, intuitive solutions to the kinds of problems that arise at work?   [ ]
- *Mental flexibility*. Can you juggle with more than one problem at a time, perhaps with conflicting information or

viewpoints to handle, and still think fast?   [ ]

- *Time management*. Do you habitually
plan your work day by day, week by week,
and make sure that priority tasks get more
of your attention than less essential ones?   [ ]
- *Proactivity*. Are you ready to take
decisions in order to make things happen
rather that sitting back and waiting for
them to happen to you?   [ ]
- *Moral courage*. Have you the guts
to choose and stick to a line of action
that may be unpopular or personally risky
because you believe it to be the right one?   [ ]
- *Resilience*. How well do you cope with
uncertainty, tension, stress, fatigue and
other people's hostility or unreasonable demands?   [ ]
- *Communication*. Are you as competent
as you feel you need to be at all the kinds of
communicating you may need to do – writing,
reading, public speaking, listening, telephoning,
interviewing, counselling, and so on?   [ ]
- *Social skills*. Can you get on
productively with other people – bosses,
colleagues, clients/customers – whether
you are being sympathetic and supportive or
are having to handle conflict or hostility
and be assertive?   [ ]
- *Self-knowledge*. Do you make a practice
of examining your own purposes, beliefs and
values and considering why you feel and behave
the way you do?   [ ]
- *The ability to learn from experience*.
Do you make a practice of reflecting on
incidents at work, weighing up the actions of
yourself and others involved, and considering
what you have learned from such incidents that
might help you handle such incidents or people
differently in future?   [ ]

Few of us will be satisfied with ourselves on all fourteen competences mentioned above. And if you aren't, don't worry. Your boss probably wouldn't be either. In fact, your boss may not even have given as much thought to such competences as you have. He or she may be less aware of his or her deficiencies than you are of yours.

Indeed, you may have a better awareness of your boss's deficiencies than he or she has. Does that put you one step ahead?

Developing Your Abilities
How can you develop whatever competences and abilities will aid you in your work? On the one hand, you can look to people to teach you. On the other hand, you can take responsibility for your own learning. (And, of course, you can combine the two approaches.)

Here are some sources from which you may be able to obtain more or less formal teaching. Which of them do you think might be able to help you with the kind of competences and abilities you want to improve?
- Coaching from your boss   [ ]
- Coaching from other colleagues   [ ]
- Sessions/courses run by your own organization   [ ]
- Local colleges/polytechnics/universities   [ ]
- Commercial training organizations   [ ]
- Professional institutions   [ ]
- Trade unions   [ ]
- Government funded schemes   [ ]
- Industry training boards   [ ]
- Employers' federations   [ ]
- Correspondence colleges   [ ]
- Open learning providers such as the Open
  University or Open College.   [ ]
- Others (what?)   . . .

And what about the following self-development or 'do-it-yourself' approaches? Which of them might be helpful to you in your self-development?

- Get together with colleagues on a regular basis to discuss problems you each have faced in your work since you last met and how you have dealt with them. [ ]
- Ask your boss to tell you about some of the most testing things he or she has to do and how he or she tackles them. [ ]
- Seek out members of staff you don't normally meet and get them to tell you about their work and the problems they face. [ ]
- Join a committee to do with some aspect of the organization's business that is unfamiliar to you. [ ]
- Ask for a temporary transfer to another branch of your organization or another section within your branch. [ ]
- Do some part-time work in another part of your organization, e.g. acting as club treasurer or helping run the crêche. [ ]
- Get friends and acquaintances elsewhere to invite you to visit their organizations. [ ]
- Join some voluntary group in your community in which you can experiment with social skills in a way you might not care to risk at work. [ ]
- Pick out someone who clearly has the abilities you want to develop; observe them in operation and get them to discuss those abilities. [ ]
- Similarly, be prepared to act as a 'rôle model' yourself for colleagues who see you as having abilities they would like to improve. (We can often learn a great deal by trying to explain our ways to other people.) [ ]
- Take time to read trade and professional journals and books that you don't normally bother with. [ ]
- Make a point of mentioning to your boss (and to other colleagues) anything you've read that may be of use or interest to them. [ ]

- Look for opportunities to speak to local
  groups, or to write articles, about your work
  and your organization.   [ ]
- Attend conferences and seminars relating
  to your work, and contribute to them.   [ ]
- Keep a journal of 'critical incidents' at
  work (there's got to be at least one a week!),
  recording what happened, how you felt and acted,
  and what you learned from it. (This could be part
  of your Work Diary.)   [ ]
- Cultivate some outside interest (anything
  from local politics to gardening) that is just as
  absorbing as your work.   [ ]
- Others (what?)   . . .

Clearly, not all the approaches above will suit everyone. But
each will be useful to someone. No doubt you and your colleagues will be able to think of other methods of your own by
which you can develop the competences and abilities you
need.

Don't set out optimistically in the hope that you can
improve on all fronts at once. Pick out one or two new
competences to improve in at a time. Wait until you feel
you have made some worthwhile progress in them before
you start giving yourself new goals to aim at. Bear all your
goals in mind, by all means, but you'd probably wear yourself
out to no good effect if you tried aiming for them all at once.

CONCLUSION

Finally, don't forget that what you are trying to do here – apart
from making yourself more capable of doing a better job and
getting more satisfaction out of it – is to manage your boss. In
particular, you are trying to manage your boss's *impression* of
you as a colleague and member of the team. So lose no opportunity to let your boss know what you are getting out of your
self-improvement activities – and let it show up clearly in the
quality of your work.

Chapter 6

The Politics of Boss-Management

Managing your boss is a political act. It is about power. You are trying to influence your boss's decisions – or to resist the effects of them, or to make those effects as congenial to you as possible.

You may also need to counteract the influence of certain other people whose wishes and interests are opposed to yours. How far you can do this depends on how much power you have and how much your boss and other people have.

How much power do you believe you have? You may already have more than you think. If you haven't enough power of your own, you'll need the support of other people with power.

If you are to manage your boss effectively, you will need to understand who has what kind of power in your organization and how it gets used. That's organizational politics.

YOU CAN'T ESCAPE POLITICS

Politics, or the struggle for power and influence, arises because we don't all think alike. Within any organization, different sections. (e.g. Production and Sales) have different interests and different priorities. Even within a section, people have different personal goals. Yours are probably different from some of your co-workers' and certainly from those of your boss.

Of course, we all have some interests and goals in common, or we couldn't work together at all. But politics arises out of our differences. We each struggle to get things as much the way we want them as possible – though we usually accept that what emerges is a compromise between what we would most like and what the other people we are working with would most like.

No one, unless you have a Great Dictator of a boss, will get it all his or her own way. But, unless we keep alive to the politics, we won't get it as much our way as it could be.

Win–Win v Win–Lose

This struggle for power does not *have* to be a vicious business of secret pacts, angry confrontations and sudden betrayals. In some organizations, folks accept, as a matter of course, that they won't see eye to eye on all issues. They are good-humoured and patient about this, and expect to spend time negotiating with one another until all are reasonably satisfied. Their aim is for everybody involved to 'win' something of what they want – rather that to produce one group, the outright 'winners', who can gloat over the 'losers'.

Other organizations, however, seem quite content to produce 'win–lose' rather than 'win–win' results. In fact, some seem to breed the mentality put into words by the writer, Gore Vidal, 'It's not enough for somebody to win; somebody else must be seen to lose.' I've known one or two bosses like that; maybe you have also.

So organizational politics can also have its dirty face. This is the scheming and self-seeking and back-biting whereby certain individuals or sections try to grab more than their fair share of what's available. They will be trying to advance their careers or win resources at the expense of their colleagues – and maybe against the best interests of the section or the organization.

POLITICS IN YOUR ORGANIZATION

What is the political climate in your organization? Is it fair and square and above board? Or is it dog eat dog, and devil take the hindmost? Or – and this is quite likely – does it differ from section to section and even from time to time, according to what is at stake? Anyway, you can't afford to be ignorant of who has got what kind of power and how you might influence things in the direction you'd like them to go.

For Good or Ill?
Power can be used for good or ill. For instance, in which of the following ways do you see power being used by your boss (B) and by your colleagues (C)?

	B	C
• To help develop the productivity and work satisfaction of individuals.	[ ]	[ ]
• To improve the contribution made by the section to the work of the organization.	[ ]	[ ]
• To overcome problems imposed on your section by people elsewhere in the organization.	[ ]	[ ]
• To obtain resources from elsewhere in the organization that are needed by your section.	[ ]	[ ]
• To block other people's reasonable and worthwhile work plans.	[ ]	[ ]
• To prevent other people advancing themselves.	[ ]	[ ]
• To make people do things that are not really in their best interests.	[ ]	[ ]
• To seek more and more power for the sake of it.	[ ]	[ ]
• To pursue personal advancement at the expense of the section or organization.	[ ]	[ ]
• To pursue personal interests at the expense of the section or organization.	[ ]	[ ]
• To advance the section's interests at the expense of the organization.	[ ]	[ ]

Maybe I'm a bit of a cynic, but I find it easier to recall foul uses of power than fair ones. Either way, I expect you'll be able to add a few examples of your own to the list above.

Power-mongering Tactics.
There is no end to the tricks people get up to when exercising power, particularly when their purposes are dubious ones. Which of the following tactics have you seen people using in your organization?

- Pretending to have less power than they do   [ ]
- Pretending to have more power than they do   [ ]
- Keeping back information from people who need it [ ]
- Distorting the information   [ ]
- Circulating slanderous gossip   [ ]
- Passing off other people's ideas as their own   [ ]
- Working to rule (e.g. go-slows)   [ ]
- Inventing new rules to restrict other people   [ ]
- Reinterpreting the existing rules to ease
  their own freedom of action   [ ]
- Empire-building   [ ]
- Espionage and infiltration of other groups   [ ]
- Fostering a climate of 'them' v 'us'   [ ]
- Forming more or less temporary cliques or
  gangs to squash other people's plans   [ ]
- Blackmailing people   [ ]
- Sabotaging other people's work or ideas   [ ]
- Physical violence (or threats of)   [ ]

Again, you'll no doubt be able to think of more specific examples of power-mongering you've come across in your own working life.

Understanding who exercises what kind of power, for what purposes, and through what tactics may be your first step towards deciding whether it is in the best interests of yourself, your section and the organization to go along with them or to fight back.

How Widespread is Power?

One point to remind ourselves of is that the boss is not the only one with power. There may be quite a few other people around with certain kinds of influence over you. For example, do you also have to cope with the expectation of:

- your boss's boss?
- other managers?
- your colleagues?
- your subordinates (if you have any)?
- people in other sections?
- customers or clients?
- other people outside the organization?

Most of us have quite a few people of influence making demands on us. We can't satisfy them all – partly because we don't have time and partly because their expectations often conflict with one another. So we may need to 'manage' all these people, besides the boss.

But managing your boss – the most powerful person making demands on you – is usually the key to getting all the others sorted out also. Unless you get your boss's firm support, other people's conflicting demands can tear you apart.

So where do you get the power to manage your boss? to answer this we must consider the various kinds of power that people do manage to get hold of.

WHERE DOES POWER COME FROM?

There are a number of kinds of power. Here I'll mention what I see as the eight main ones:

1. *Resource power*. You've got this sort of power if you are in control of resources. These resources may be money, equipment, spaces in the car park – indeed, anything that is desired by other people and which they

can obtain only if they satisfy you in some way.

2. *Information power*. This kind of power comes from having access to inside information – information that most other people don't have (or don't have yet). The information may, for example, be about what is going on 'behind the scenes' in your section or organization or it may simply be plans of your own that you have not yet shared with others.

   Whatever form it takes, it enables you to make better-informed decisions and to act more effectively than people who are not yet in the know. And people who know you to be a source of such information may do you favours in order to gain access to it.

3. *Position power*. This power will be yours purely because you have a recognized rôle and title within the organization. It may not cut much ice on its own. Some people may be impressed by the fact that you are called Chief this or Senior that, while others won't give a damn – not unless you can back it up with one of the other forms of power mentioned in this list.

4. *Proxy power*. Yours because you represent some person or group whom the people you are dealing with dare not go against – e.g. 'Speaking on behalf of the workforce/the management/the shareholders/the users' group . . .'

5. *Expert power*. This kind of power will be yours if people believe that you know more than they do about one or more aspects of the work you are doing together – accountancy, nursing, house-building, or whatever. People will therefore be inclined to act so you suggest, because they trust your judgement.

   Strictly speaking, you don't *really* have to know more than they do. It is only necessary that they believe you do. In deciding whether people are worthy of expert-power, we have to decide whether they truly do know more than we do or are merely shooting us a line.

Needless to say, you may be able to influence people in one area of work, because of your expertise; yet those same people will disregard your suggestions in another area because you are not recognized as an expert there.

6. *Personality power*. Yours because you have (at least for the time being) some kind of charisma or self-confidence or sense of mission that persuades people to go along with you. You influence them with your personal enthusiasm or ebullience – encouraging them and making *them* feel more capable of achieving something they believe to be worthwhile. If your enthusiasm wanes, or the achievements are slow in coming, this form of power may be short-lasting.

7. *Physical power*. Perhaps you have a powerful physique or deep and resonant voice? Or maybe you tend to move in close on people or loom over them, or otherwise dominate them with your body language? Or maybe you just exude an aroma of self-confidence and strength (like some sort of chemical, perhaps)? Maybe people have just the slightest suspicion – though you've never been known to raise so much as your voice, let alone your fist, in anger – that you might be capable of physically flattening any opposition. Whatever the secret, it somewhat unnerves or intimidates people and makes them willing to defer to your wishes.

8. *Favour power*. You'll have this kind of power if you have done favours for powerful people in the past. When the chips are down and you need help, you can call on them to repay by lending you *their* power.

As the saying goes, 'they owe you one'. How willing they may be to repay will perhaps depend on whether they think you still capable of doing them good or harm in future. The Mafia boss in *The Godfather*, I remember, seemed to have relatively little trouble persuading people to repay favours he had done them many years before.

Which of these kinds of power do you actually have? Which kinds does your boss have? By definition, she or he will have more power than you – especially resource power perhaps. But maybe you have some kinds of power your boss does not. For example, she or he may sometimes have to bow to your expertise, even though you can't put it to full effect unless she or he gives you the resources to do so.

Maybe some of the other demanding people we listed a page or two back will also have some of these kinds of power. What kinds of power can you line up to counterbalance theirs?

HOW TO OBTAIN MORE POWER

The only way of resisting other people's power is to acquire more of your own – or at least make maximum use of what you've already got. There are many hints in the list above as to how you might do this – get control of resources, gather information, become an acknowledged expert, do people favours and so on.

Here are some more specific suggestions. Which of them do you feel might be appropriate to your situation?

- Make a point of finding out who are the powerful people around your section and elsewhere in the organization who might be able to help you at some time or other. Obviously, you will include your own boss in this category, but look further afield. He or she is not the only one with power. And don't just consider managers. Some apparently lowly people may have, for instance, information power – e.g. typists, caretakers, the tea lady, the boy who comes round with the mail.

- Find out what each of these people would welcome by way of 'favours' – e.g. respect, someone to discuss their domestic troubles with, more resources, help with difficult bosses or subordinates, or whatever.

- Provide such favours where you feel it is not unethical (or disloyal to other colleagues) to do so. At all events, avoid antagonizing such people unless you feel some greater purpose is at stake. Don't make enemies.

- Do good turns for people whenever you can. And don't dismiss anyone as of no account and not worth your time. Even if helping all and sundry is not something you're inclined to do anyway, consider this: even the most unlikely recipient of your favours may one day come up with just the help that will save you in your hour of need.

  Besides, as the old saying has it: 'Be nice to people you pass on your way up – you may meet them again on your way down.'

- Join the unofficial 'networks' of staff (the sports teams, the community service group, the drama club, etc.) that cut across the formal hierarchy of the organization. These will give you access to inside information that may not be available to other people in your section – not even to your boss.

  They will also present you with new people you can do good turns for, as outlined above. Thus your potential favour power will be increasing.

- Sometimes you will most effectively gain more power by collaborating with other people. Often these will be colleagues in your own section. Together, you will have more power to move the boss than any one of you would if acting alone.

  Or there may be staff in other sections with whom you can find common interests. Do deals with other individuals or groups who will give you support in what you are after, provided you are willing to do the same for them.

- Persuade people to support you by making out a good case for what you want done. You may do this in terms of how the organization or the section will benefit – but usually it will also be necessary to show what is in it for the person you are trying to convince. Even the manager responsible for a section may not be persuaded to support you unless you make clear how he or she, as well as the section, will benefit. Some won't worry at all about benefits to the section so long as they see what's in it for them.

Make your case in writing and/or face to face, as seems most appropriate. If a particular individual seems resistant to your arguments, arrange for them to be approached by one or more people he or she respects who happen to be your supporters. That is, use your existing supporters to help win you new ones.

- Volunteer for the kinds of tasks and projects that give you control of more resources and/or access to more powerful people and/or enable you to develop more expertise. Each new piece of work you undertake is a potential source of more power. The list of eight types of power I described earlier should help you decide what might be available to you in your organization.

  With each new increase in your power, ask yourself how it can be used to gain you yet more power. For example, suppose you go on a course that gives you more expert power. Can you persuade your boss to make the most of your new expertise by delegating to you a new project that allows you to control more resources?

- Let people see that you use what power you have in an open, responsible and public-spirited fashion – and not to advance your own interests at the expense of others. Above all, don't be greedy. Don't expect to have everything your own way. Other people's goals and interests will often be just as valid as yours.

  Your aim should be to get a *fair* share of what power is available, not to stop your colleagues from scoring. Wherever possible, go for a 'win–win' result rather than a 'win–lose'. (Apart from the ethics of it, if your winning alienates your colleagues, they may be at pains to ensure that you lose something important as soon as possible also – 'lose–lose'.)

Where other people are seeking power to use in a responsible fashion, give them the same kind of support you would hope for from others. But where they are seeking power or abusing it to pursue dubious ends, don't hesitate to undermine them by bringing their political jiggery-pokery out into the open.

SEEKING POWER FROM YOUR BOSS

Your boss probably possesses more power than anyone else with whom you have regular dealings. Your boss is likely to have control of resources, or privileged information, or bags of personality, or is well-regarded by even more powerful people in the organization. For all these reasons and more, he or she has a certain amount of 'clout'. He or she can persuade people to do things his or her way. This is boss-power.

Power Sharing

An important element of managing your boss is getting him or her to share some of that power with you. You'll probably get quite a long way in this by applying some of the ideas discussed elsewhere in this book. In particular, you need to agree with your boss exactly what your job is, do it well, and make sure your boss notices that you are doing it well. 'Impression management' is the name of this particular game.

The more your boss respects you and the work you are doing, the more likely he or she is to let you influence his or her decision-making. Indeed, he or she may:

- listen to your advice or suggestions;
- delegate more decision-making to you;
- share important information with you;

- give you more and more freedom to do things your way without being constantly checked up on;
- allow your some control over resources that he or she is ultimately responsible for, and so on.

In short, you may get *proxy power* by being asked more and more to act on behalf of your boss – with less and less interference.

The Importance of Trust

All the depends, of course, on how far your boss can trust you. Is your boss convinced that he or she can rely on you? Are you seen as a supporter and not some kind of threat?

Your boss may be under the impression that you see him or her as an obstacle in the way of getting the boss's job for yourself. Or he or she may think you are both competing for some better job elsewhere in the organization. If so, he or she is unlikely to share power with you or do anything at all that enables you to shine.

If you see your boss more as an adviser and mentor than as someone you are competing with for advancement, then it's as well to make this clear. Ideally, you should aim to be working *with* your boss rather than *for* your boss. In some cases, admittedly, you may end up working *against* your boss. But make sure your boss does not think this is your intention when it is not.

And how far can you trust your boss? Does your boss appear to have a genuine supportive interest in you as an individual? Does he or she show signs of wanting to help you make your work as satisfying as possible and enable you to learn and develop as far as you want to?

Or does your boss pay no attention to your needs and wishes? Is he or she interested merely in whether the work quotas are completed and the organization's rules and regulations obeyed to the letter? Perhaps you're just another anonymous cog in the wheel as far as he or she is concerned. Worse still, has he or she got a down on you – maybe for no good reason you know of? Is it apparent to you that he or she has got favourites (which don't include you) and they are going to get all the special treatment that's going?

Knowing About Your Boss

You may have noticed that most of my advice in this book seems to make certain assumptions about your boss. Particularly, I have mostly written as though your boss is reasonably confident, rational and well-meaning. For example, she or he:

1. Is confident of her or his own managerial skills and the extent of her or his freedom to exercise power within the organization.
2. Has clear goals, objectives and purposes.
3. Can obtain all the information she or he needs to make sensible decisions.
4. Makes decisions in the light of what is best for the section and the organization as a whole, as well as for herself or himself.
5. Is committed to making the most of the talents of the people who form her or his section.
6. Deals fairly with individuals and is willing to listen to their comments and suggestions.
7. Is honest, straightforward and honourable in dealings with you and your colleagues.

And so on.

Now, you may say 'Fair enough; that sounds more or less like my boss.' or you may already be hooting with laughter at the thought of the paranoid, secretive, indecisive tyrant you call your boss developing any such admirable qualities as these.

So, how you interpret my thoughts on the politics of boss-management is up to you. Only you know what will be necessary with the boss in your life. If your boss is basically straightforward and you know where you are with him or her, then you can afford to be equally open and above board in your efforts to manage him or her. If, on the other hand, your boss is a dubious character, perhaps much practised in the dirty tricks department of organizational politics, then you may feel compelled to be equally devious.

How long you'll be able to live with yourself if you do have to work 'against' the boss in this way, is a matter for you and your sense of self-respect to sort out. It can be pretty soul-destroying. (The final chapter of this book contains a few thoughts on what to do should the strain of dealing with an impossible boss become just too much.)

So, in managing your boss, you need to keep in mind what kind of boss you've got. As we discussed in Chapter 3, the more you know about your boss the better. An approach that goes down well with one person might fail hopelessly with another – or even with that first person on a different occasion.

Know Your Own Purposes

But you also need to keep in mind your own *purposes*. Are you, for example, trying:

- to get the boss's support for something you want to do?
- to keep the boss from interfering with something you are already doing?
- to discourage the boss from foisting some unwanted task on you?

Or what other purposes? In any encounter with your boss – whether face-to-face, in writing, or on the telephone – you may need to think fast about what you'd like out of it. Other-wise, you may get side-tracked and give away more than you gain.

☆   ☆   ☆

So much for the political background. In Chapter 7 we come down to the everyday practicalities involved in managing your boss.

Chapter 7

Practical Boss-Management

In Chapter 6 we considered the wider political background to managing your boss. In this chapter we must come down to the everyday practicalities.

A prime aim in boss-management is to get your boss's support for what you want to do. But in order to win your boss's support, you must convince your boss that he or she can rely on yours. So that's where we'll begin – with giving and getting support. Then we'll discuss a number of other useful tactics.

HOW TO SHOW YOUR SUPPORT

Find out how best to support your boss. This is basically a matter of doing your job well. But there's more to it than that. If you follow the spirit of Chapter 3 – and work on getting to know your boss – you'll learn of other areas where he or she can most benefit from what you can offer.

Get Your Boss to Rely on You
Encourage your boss to talk to you about his or her problems. Volunteer to help with them where you can. Bring to your boss's attention any strengths you may have that can compensate for his or her weaknesses – e.g. 'Computers are one of my hobbies, so if you want someone to sort the programming out, just let me know.'

Demonstrate how you can be a valuable, perhaps indispensable, ally in achieving his or her goals. Make clear how you can help your boss to overcome anything that he or she fears or is anxious about – e.g. 'I don't mind going to sort out that mob in the laboratory if you're too busy.'

Learn to anticipate your boss's needs, priorities and expectations. Don't wait to be told. Bring things to his or her attention, if necessary – e.g. 'I thought you might want to reply to this letter about us in the local paper.'

When your boss does put his or her trust in you, keep your promises. Whatever jobs he or she delegates to you, see them through to completion. Don't turn in a half-baked effort with all the tricky bits left for your boss to sort out.

Speak No Evil

Speak well of your boss to others – assuming he or she, in general, deserves it. It's easy to join in a general rubbishing of your boss along with your colleagues, even when you know in your heart that it's not your boss's fault that someone elsewhere in the organization is screwing up your whole section.

I know we all look for convenient scapegoats to blame our trouble on. Usually, however, they get to hear you've been bad-mouthing them. And you probably can't afford for your boss to learn you've been calling him or her names. At least be as loyal to your boss as your boss is to you.

Supporting by Challenging

Loyalty doesn't mean you have to agree with every word your boss utters when the two of you are together on your own. You don't have to be a yes-person. Think twice about your self-esteem before you go along with any of your boss's statements that offend your sense of what's right. Is getting what you want out of the boss worth buttoning your lip for? Does the end justify the means?

If your boss can't take an outright rejection of his or her views, then you may have to satisfy yourself with a face-saving formula like that used by subordinates of the newspaper tycoon in Evelyn Waugh's *Black Mischief* – 'Up to a point, Lord Copper.'

But very often, the best form of support you can give your

boss is to *challenge* his or her views. If your boss trusts you, he or she may want to see you as a 'sounding board'. For instance, he or she may want to 'think aloud' in your company, tossing out new ideas to get your reactions. His or her hope will be that you'll help identify any snags that need sorting out before he or she risks putting those ideas to more senior (and more powerful) colleagues.

So, you may support your boss by saying: 'Have you considered what the union's attitude would be?' or 'Wouldn't that be likely to go against the recent legislation?' or 'Could we possibly get it through the committee system in time?' Of course, you may also be able to balance your negative comments by positive suggestions as to how the snags might be overcome.

Don't Alienate Your Colleagues

In supporting your boss, take care not to alienate your colleagues. You don't want to get mistrusted as the boss's pet or a running dog of the organization.

Be as open as possible about what you are doing and try to support your colleagues also in whatever efforts they are making to manage the boss. Admittedly, there are some situations – e.g. when two of you are competing for the only available promotion – where this may not be possible.

HOW TO GET YOUR BOSS'S SUPPORT

The essence of managing your boss is to show her or him that you can be relied on – not just to do your job but also to provide her or him with indispensable support in doing hers or his. You are then in a strong position to expect your boss's support in return.

You'll know what sort of proposals or requests you might want to put to your boss. These will be different at different times. Maybe you'll want new responsibilities, a change of policy, new equipment, a rise in salary.

Which of your proposals is your boss likely to warm to?
Which is he or she most free to support without having to
go, in turn, for support from his or her boss?

Attractive Proposals
How can you make your proposals as attractive as possible?
Ideally, you should be able to show that they will benefit not
just you but also the section – and above all, perhaps, the
boss. For example, 'We need this new computer, because
I'll be able to draw on a wider range of data and provide *you*
with more up-to-date statistics when you are trying to get the
section additional resources.'

How to Propose?
Find out how your boss likes proposals to be presented, e.g. in
a written document or in a leisurely face-to-face discussion.
Maybe it's both. I once had a boss who would only look at a
written proposal if her staff had first managed to convince her
in a one-minute oral presentation that the subject was really
worth her attention. And even then she wouldn't consider
more than one side of paper!

When to Propose?
When is the best time to approach your boss? First thing
in the morning? Over lunch? Mid-afternoon? Are Monday
mornings ideal and Friday afternoons hopeless? Is he or she
most receptive after a new project has been announced or a
lengthy job successfully completed?

Look out for occasions when your boss is in a particularly
buoyant frame of mind – perhaps because he or she has just
been given a pay rise or has won a big new contract. If you've
got a proposal simmering on your back burner, now might be
the very best time to turn up the heat.

Don't Go Off Half-Cock
You won't always get an opportunity to choose your time, of
course. Circumstances will sometimes 'put you on the spot',
dictating that you make your case right now or risk losing all

chance of making it in the future. If your boss is clearly not in a listening mood, you may nevertheless decide to take that risk. If you do, you may need to work extra hard to manufacture a better occasion later.

It is especially easy to get drawn into making your pitch at a particular moment merely because it ties in with something else you and the boss happen to be talking about. 'While we're on the subject, I've been meaning to ask you . . .,' you may hear yourself saying. Think twice before you do. Don't spoil your chances by raising the matter if your boss seems less than reasonably receptive – e.g. because she or he has just been sounding off at you about the subject that brought your proposal to mind! Leave it for a more promising occasion.

Where to Propose?

Likewise, what is the best *situation* in which to tackle your boss? Will he or she be most amenable in the office, or if you go out to the pub together at lunchtime, or if you take a walk together around the park?

And is your boss best tackled on his or her own? Or should you try to put your case while your boss's boss and maybe other managers (preferably those you know would support you) are also present? Indeed, can you put it best on your own, or do you need to be one of a deputation – 'Speaking on behalf of the entire production staff . . . '?

Some General Rules

All such judgements you make about the best timing and the best situation will depend on how well you know your boss. The better you get to know his or her mind, the better you'll be able to manage the occasion.

So too with the way you actually put your proposal or seek your boss's support. Here are a few skeleton rules. You can put the flesh on them according to what you think your boss will go for:

Show your boss what she or he can *gain* from what you are proposing. Maybe you can present it as a solution to a problem that she or he has been concerned about. Maybe you can show how it will enable your boss to demonstrate improved productivity in the section. Maybe you can make clear how it will help stave off some sort of threat from another part of the organization.

You know what your boss desires and fears. Where possible, present your proposals or requests with these in mind. You may have to remind your boss of the potentially embarrassing consequences of *not* giving you the kind of support you are looking for. Don't pull any punches. But don't overstate the case either – or not if there's the faintest chance your boss will believe you've done so.

Whatever you do, don't try to wangle your boss into a situation where it becomes clear that you can gain what you want only at her or his expense. Ensure at least that your boss takes no risk for you without some prospect of gain. Such a gain does not have to be immediate, but it does need to be in the easily foreseeable future.

Remind your boss, as casually or forcefully as necessary, of all the support she or he is getting from you. Ensure your boss appreciates how essential it is that this support continues undiminished.

Present your proposals or requests in such a way that your boss can contribute to them. She or he should feel some sort of 'ownership' in them. Perhaps you can even show how your proposal arises out of some earlier ideas put forward by your boss. Maybe she or he wrote something or made some remarks that could be said to have inspired your present proposals. If you *can* say so, say so.

Some people think the ideal would be to get your boss to sell back to you your own idea – under the illusion that it is her or his own. Well, maybe. You may have to get used to sitting in meetings listening to your boss trotting out your carefully wrought schemes as if they were her or his own personal visions.

It's difficult to know how far to go along with this, however. You may win the battle – of getting your proposal adopted. But you may lose the wider 'war' – by not gaining proper credit for your creativity. Perhaps it all depends on *what kind* of proposal you're seeking support for.

Using Your Boss's Ideas

What if your boss suggests changes to your proposals? Above all, make it clear that you are taking them seriously.

If your boss makes suggestions that seem practicable and fit in with your proposals, welcome them with honest acclaim. Let your boss see that you are ready to build them into your proposals. These will now be jointly 'owned' by you and your boss. She or he will then be likely to give you more whole-hearted backing.

Be open also to the possibility that your boss will make an altogether *better* proposal – one that will offer you more than you had thought to ask for. Your boss may have her or his own reasons for wanting to give you more encouragement than you could have expected. If so, make the most of it. Ask yourself why, and whether you can look for even more support in the near future.

But what if your boss is less co-operative? Suppose she or he makes suggestions that are not practicable or might prevent you getting what you are after. Your first step might be to get her or him to discuss the implications of those suggestions. In particular, try to get your boss to see the ways she or he might *lose* if your proposals were so changed.

With luck, your boss may come round to acknowledging that her or his suggested changes would not be an improvement on your proposals. Though you may need to prompt your boss with some remark that allows her or him to withdraw the suggestion without losing face.

Some bosses have the kind of self-confidence that enables them quite happily to argue and 'lose' a point of view with a member of their staff. You should know whether you've got one of these – or one of the other sort, who would be mortified, and therefore may need your help in saving face. As they say in the negotiation business: 'Always leave your "opponents" the price of the bus-fare home.'

Dealing With Objections

Of course your boss may put forward some fundamental objections to your proposal – or insist upon radical changes that are not at all congenial to you. Ideally, you should try to think of all the objections or radical modifications your boss might suggest *before* you present your proposal. (Rather like sales staff do in anticipating the ways that potential customers might resist buying what they have to offer.)

In so far as you can do this – and again it depends on how well you know how your boss's mind works – you should be able to *rehearse* the arguments that are most likely to overcome her or his resistance.

If your boss does raise objections, argue your case as clearly and strongly as you can. Keep in mind the vital question: what's in it for your boss? But don't be belligerent or fanatical about it. Otherwise your boss may be likely to respond in kind – and that probably won't get you the result you are looking for. But don't beg, plead or moan, either. Be neither a raging bull nor a whingeing wet. Show that you are rational and can keep your emotions out of the discussion, even if it's a struggle.

Don't admit defeat immediately – unless your boss really has identified some snag colossal enough to make you curse yourself for not having noticed it earlier. Maybe you can argue a case that will convince your boss off the top of your head; maybe not. Don't try if you're not sure of your ground.

Be prepared to tell your boss that her or his suggestions require you to go away and think through their implications. Don't let her or him think that you've been defeated or have come along with a scheme that was only half-baked. It's more that you respect her or his ideas too much to treat them lightly.

If you see your arguments are making no impression on your boss, retreat with dignity. Go away and think some more about your proposal and just why your boss objected to it. Then come back another day with a modified and perhaps more acceptable version.

DON'T BUG YOUR BOSS

The most basic rule in effective boss-management is to avoid making difficulties for your boss. Don't give him or her any cause to worry about your work – and therefore to start interfering with it. Don't bother the boss with minor problems you can sort out yourself (or with the help of colleagues).

If your boss is going to get to hear about problems you are having, make sure he or she hears it from you first. And get in quick. Don't risk your boss being embarrassed – perhaps even with his or her boss – by having to admit ignorance of a crisis (caused by you) that is just about to hit the section.

Managing Your Errors

If things are going badly wrong, tell your boss what has happened. But choose your moment, and think about how you are going to raise the matter. Be ready with your suggestions as to how things might be put right.

Do you need more time, more resources, extra staff, or what? Invite your boss's views and suggestions, but don't act as though you expect him or her to solve the problem for you. Where possible, try to find something positive in the situation that you and your boss can be relieved and optimistic about. (First the bad news, now the good news?)

Don't waste time on excuses or on trying to find scapegoats. If you think the boss is to blame – e.g. by having set you impossible deadlines – keep the thought to yourself. Stick to the facts, and let your boss see for himself or herself that the fault is not yours (if it isn't).

If the fault is yours, be honest and open about it. Admit your mistakes. Nobody's perfect. Don't insult your boss's intelligence by trying to mislead – especially if he or she can clearly see that's what you're doing. A brief rollocking may be better for your relationship in the long run – better, that is, than getting yourself the reputation of being devious and untrustworthy.

But try to steer your boss into planning for the future rather than moaning about your past mistakes. Make clear that you have thought about the experience and are capable of *learning* from what has happened. Maybe your boss will have some hints and tips to help you. Leave your boss feeling confident that you see better ways of tackling such situations in the future and are unlikely to trouble him or her with such a problem again.

WATCH WHAT YOU SAY

Or, to put it more delicately, consider your Information Control. As I said in Chapter 6, information is power. In so far as you have information that your boss, as yet, does not, you may have a certain amount of power over him or her.

You may not always see the need to tell your boss everything you know. If your relations with your boss are friendly, open and supportive, then you will expect to exchange whatever information might be to the other's advantage. If you have any reason to mistrust your boss, you may feel otherwise.

The Perils of Telling
Telling your boss what you are doing, for example, may give him or her undue encouragement to interfere with those activities. Better, perhaps, to wait until the job is done and then report – when it's too late for the boss to pester you to do it differently. This is a peril you often come across when your boss is someone who has done your sort of work in the past.

A similar peril may arise when you are doing some very specialist work which your boss has little or no knowledge of but is nevertheless responsible for. If your boss is not too secure, he or she may be forever breathing nervously down your neck in the hope of convincing himself or herself that nothing's going wrong.

You may need to fend off such bosses by blinding them with science. You may need to use your 'expert power' to convince them that they can feel quite safe (and much less embarrassed by their own ignorance) if they just leave you to get on with it. Give them enough information to reassure them that they won't be left with egg on their face – and get them off your back.

Think twice before you say what is in your mind. Now may not be the best time to win your boss's support. And you may be able to think of better arguments, given time. At least consider the likely results of your words and how you might modify them to get what you desire.

Treasure Your Information

Always remember the value of information. Don't give it away – unless you absolutely trust your boss to be equally open with you. Consider how you might obtain something in exchange for it – if only further information you might find useful yourself.

Knowing your boss, you may decide that certain information would be best kept from him or her, anyway. Or at least that you'd do well not to be the bearer of the news. His or her hobbyhorses and prejudices may be so overpowering that you'd be the one to suffer the tumult of his or her wrath.

Again, you may have a boss who is irrational when it comes to making decisions, or perhaps he or she is nervous about making them at all. Maybe he or she is unduly antagonistic towards certain people in the organization or is unduly fearful of making mistakes and offending powerful individuals.

If you are trying to influence such a boss's decisions, or get support for something you want to do, you may again decide that certain information you have might be better kept to yourself. The only way to get a rational decision, or perhaps any decision at all, may be to focus your boss's attention. This you may do by omitting to mention information that might cause him or her to do something silly (or nothing at all).

Too Much v Too Little

I am not talking here about telling lies – or even about what, in government circles, is called 'the dissemination of disinformation'. My point is simply that, if your boss is 'difficult' to deal with, saying all you know may often make him or her even more difficult. Too much of the wrong kind of information may make your boss impossible.

But information control is not all negative – not just a matter of shielding your boss from facts that might complicate matters. More positively, you may have to bring your boss's attention to *additional* information that might help him or her overcome doubts or reservations. Maybe you can find experts or specialists whose opinions the boss will respect – or just present your boss with appropriately authoritative writings from books and journals.

DON'T BE A PUSHOVER

People don't much value things they get too easily. This includes your time and services. So, how do you reply if your boss (or anyone else) asks you to do something above and beyond the call of duty? Do you immediately say 'No problem' or 'That's easy' or 'It'll be a pleasure'?

Well, perhaps you do. It all depends on your relationship with the person asking. Would they be equally obliging if you asked them for a favour? If so, and what they are asking is not too disruptive, you may indeed be happy to do it.

What's Your Price?

If not, you may be less ready to leap into action. You may wonder what sort of 'price' (or favour) you may be able to extract from them by putting yourself out as they request. At least you will expect them to acknowledge that you *have* put yourself out for them.

If you don't obtain at least this recognition, then you may get taken for granted in future. People will assume that you must have plenty of time on your hands or that you don't much care what you do. Many more odds and sods of jobs will be landed on you. Or you'll be drafted around from pillar to post, filling in for other people, or clearing up their messes.

Resisting Unwelcome Demands

There are numerous ways of resisting unwanted new demands. Which of the following might you sometimes find practicable?

- Make a point of not being available
  whenever the proposer suggests getting into
  a detailed discussion of the work he or she
  wants done.   [ ]
- Agree to 'take it on board', but
  don't say when you'll actually do anything
  about it.   [ ]
- Agree to take on something similar
  to what the proposer is suggesting – but
  reinterpret it to better suit your own purposes.
  (Send the proposer a suitable memo recording
  what you have agreed to do.)   [ ]
- Point out problems and anomalies in
  the proposal, causing the proposer to
  go away and do some more work on it.   [ ]
- Scupper the proposal completely,
  preferably through the comments of some
  'impartial' expert who owes you a favour,
  by drawing attention to a fundamental flaw.   [ ]
- Enthuse about how appropriate the
  proposal would have been at some earlier
  time, or will be at some time in the future,
  but regret the various factors that would make
  it impossible to implement just at present.   [ ]
- Point out how some other individual or
  section within the organization would be better
  placed to carry out the work and/or would
  be deeply offended if they were not offered

it. (With this one, you may need to 'wind up' the individual or section concerned to the point where they really would feel they might be missing something if the work were not offered to them.)   [ ]

- In certain circumstances, a controlled tantrum may be in order: 'How can you think of piling this on me/us, when you know the pressure I'm/we're already under.'   [ ]
- Simply refuse to do the work.   [ ]

When to Say NO

As the last item above indicates, you may sometimes need to learn to say NO. This is easier, of course, if the person asking has little or no direct power over you – is not your boss, for example. It is still very difficult for some people, however, especially perhaps for women.

The trick is to make your refusal immediate, firm and convincing. You don't have time, the resources aren't available, or your boss (or your union) wouldn't allow it.

Of course, if the person asking is really keen, you may allow yourself to be persuaded – as a very special 'one-off' favour, for which you will expect a favour in return (now or later). But if you really don't want to do it, and you'll lose nothing by refusing, don't do it.

Sympathize with the predicament of the person who is asking you by all means. But don't *apologize* that your time is so heavily booked up that you can't help them out. Next time they ask you, they'll perhaps remember the value of your time and come offering you a better deal.

Saying NO to the boss may be more difficult. But it can (and often must) be done. Otherwise, some bosses will load you up with all kinds of awful jobs and have you slaving away long after everyone else has finished for the day.

With the boss, as with anyone else, you need to decide whether you might gain more by taking on the new work than you'd lose by refusing it. Maybe there is some obvious advantage to you – e.g. a visit to foreign parts or a chance to gain some potentially valuable expertise. But you may still want to be critical about what the boss is (or seems to be) offering you:

- why does he/she want you to do it?
- what's in it for him/her?
- what does he/she think might be in it for you?
- what (or what else) do you think might be in it for you?
- what might you lose by doing it?
- what might you lose by refusing it?
- on balance, is it worth doing?
- how much can you persuade your boss to 'pay' (not least with a sense of dependence on you) if you take on the work?

Be Wary of 'Gifts'

Keep especially critical if what you are being offered sounds like something you might be expected to value – e.g. a *promotion*. Of course, it may be just what you're after – more money, more resources, more power, more freedom to work in your own way.

On the other hand, what you're being offered may make new and unwelcome demands on you without offering anything much that you would value in return. Remember the Peter Principle, which says that organizations tend to promote people to the point at which they become incompetent – and also to the point where they lose the satisfaction they previously had in their work.

If your boss wants to promote you and you see some advantage in what he or she proposes, don't immediately fall to licking his or her boots. Discuss the pros and cons of the proposal with appropriate gravity, and squeeze out as many perks as you think the system will allow. You may rarely get a better chance.

Similarly, if your boss is merely asking you to take on a new assignment rather than offering a promotion. Even if you see some advantage in doing the work, you may prefer not to share this opinion with your boss. You may prefer to play hard to get. You may remind your boss of your already tight work schedule, make a big issue of what sort of priority he or she wants you to give to the new work, and which of your current work he or she would prefer to see you delay or abandon in order to fit in the new work.

Costs and Extra Benefits

You may also feel obliged to remind your boss of the likely *costs* involved – extra equipment or facilities needed, over-time payments, disappointed clients or customers for work that will have to be delayed, and so on. Other people in the organization (including your boss's boss) may be less than pleased. And, of course, there may be other people in the organization who could do the job as well as you, anyway.

If, in spite of these manifold difficulties, your boss still wants you to do the work, what is your 'price'? Now may be the time to press for that new equipment, or an extra staff member, or control of a slice of your boss's budget. Only with that kind of extra resource is there any hope of your being able to satisfy your boss's requirements. Come to that, maybe a promotion will be necessary after all, if you are to have sufficient 'rank' to inspire confidence among those with whom you must collaborate in getting the job done!

Measuring Your Promises

Even so, you may decide not to be too gung-ho and can-do about it. You may feel your boss will be somewhat suspicious if his or her granting of extra resources suddenly makes the impossible super-easy. Besides which, you are unlikely to be given all the resources you suggested were necessary.

So, you may make a point of promising less than you really expect to be able to deliver. You say you'll do your best to finish the job by the end of the week or to produce at least 75% of what your boss is asking for.

But, lo and behold, by pulling out all the stops, you manage to finish by Thursday or produce the full 100%. And make sure your boss realizes how grateful he or she should be – and perhaps how you would like that gratitude expressed.

Don't be obstructive. Always be sympathetic. You want

your boss to feel he or she can rely on you to do everything in your power to support him or her. But he or she must realize that, in order for you to be able to provide additional support, he or she may need to provide you with *additional* power.

Dealing With Change

There are times when playing hard to get is the very best thing you could do for your boss. I am thinking of those times where your boss is being persuaded (probably by his or her boss, or even someone yet further up in the organization) to introduce *change* into your section.

Your boss may or may not believe in the value of these changes. In fact, he or she may not even understand them or have thought much about them.

You may be doing him or her a favour if, instead of simply agreeing to implement the change, you raise questions like these:

- What exactly is the change meant to accomplish, e.g. in terms of increased productivity or improved quality of working life?
- How different is it from what we are doing already?
- Has it been tried successfully elsewhere?
- Has it been unsuccessful elsewhere (or here in the past)?
- How can we be sure it will work?
- Is it ethical?
- Will it serve some people's interests at the expense of others'?
- Is it based on untested theory or speculation?
- Is it just another fashion or 'flavour of the month'?
- Will it solve any problem worth solving?
- Might it create more problems than it solves?
- It is likely to be cost-effective?
- Does the section have an appropriate budget?
- Might it antagonize staff/unions/customers, etc?

With your support, your boss may summon up the courage to resist the changes, or at least get them modified so that they better suit the needs of your section. (And your own purposes, of course.)

GET IT IN WRITING

Perhaps the most useful bit of advice I was given on joining one organization was 'If you disagree with somebody, make sure you put it in writing. Then at least they won't be able to say you never told them.' One thing I now want to add: If you've agreed something with somebody, put that in writing too.

Record Your Agreements

The fact is, the words of our bosses are too often written on the wind. They are uttered, they may be meant at the time (though they may be understood differently by the utterer and the hearer), but then they vanish into thin air. An essential tactic in managing your boss is to get a record of those words. I'm not suggesting you bug his or her office, though no doubt this is common practice in some organizations. I'm just talking about pieces of paper.

In previous chapters I've mentioned the importance of having written job descriptions or work plans – with both you and your boss having a copy. So too with whatever you may agree between you as a result of a performance appraisal.

But, really, anything of importance you agree with your boss is worth making a written record of. You may wait for your boss to write you a note or a memo. This may be the polite and understood thing to do in some organizations. But it does give your boss the opportunity to recast your agreement, however slightly, in terms more convenient to her or his viewpoint.

You may prefer to seize the initiative and get your interpretation in first, as a pre-emptive strike. Do you want, perhaps, to write a little more leeway into your agreed duties or objectives than your boss might have intended? An early 'confirming' memo may enable you to do so. If your boss notices anything she or he disagrees with in your 'record of the meeting', then you may receive a suggested correction by return mail. If there is a real disagreement between you as to what was 'agreed', then you may need to meet and resolve it – without resorting to a memo war!

Record Your Doubts

It is equally important, if not more so, to put on record any doubts or reservations you may have about a project – especially if it's one you feel your boss has landed you with against your better judgement. You may even send copies of such a memo to your boss's boss and/or to other people around the organization.

Such memo-writing can seem a drag, but it can also save your bacon. Bosses may forget (purposely or otherwise) what was agreed or not agreed. And if someone's head is going to be on the chopping block for an unwise (and unrecorded) decision it's more likely to be yours than your boss's. Besides which, bosses do fall under the proverbial bus, or at least move on, perhaps to other organizations, leaving no-one to back up your story of what was agreed or disagreed.

Memos and Impression Management

Finally, don't overlook the value of the memo in the art and craft of 'impression management'. Keep up a steady stream of memos to your boss on matters that are likely to seem important to her or him. One or two a week may be about the target to aim for.

There should always be some sort of progress or achievement to report, some new challenge or opportunity to bring to the boss's attention. It may be merely a press cutting with a 'Thought you might find this of interest' scribbled in the margin. With anything extra juicy, or particularly likely to reflect credit on yourself, you may also want to send a copy of your memo to your boss's boss.

ASSERT YOURSELF

As should be clear from this and previous chapters, managing your bosses will often demand that you stand up for yourself. ('Don't be a pushover.') 'Assertiveness' they call this, nowadays. This does not mean aggressiveness. You are not expected to crush your bosses with physical power – shouting them down or treating them to a knuckle sandwich.

Assertion v Aggression

Rather, assertiveness means acting as though your ideas and feelings are as important – and as much worth paying attention to – as your boss's. You don't deny your boss's rights, or anyone else's, for that matter. That would be aggressive. But you know you have rights too, and you make sure the other person knows what you believe those rights to be.

If you get aggressive with other people, they will usually get aggressive back. Instead of a rational discussion, you end up with a slanging match – both parties perhaps saying things they regret afterwards – and nothing gets accomplished. Lose – lose. But if you are non-assertive, the other party never gets to hear your point of view – perhaps never even realizes yours is different from theirs. So you still lose.

How to be Assertive

Being assertive demands that you keep calm and rational, straightforwardly describing your position in the confidence that your boss (or whoever) owes you the courtesy of listening just as calmly and rationally. So, when you need to be assertive with your boss:

A. Try to make your own appointment to see him or her, rather than waiting to be summoned. (But don't just storm in unannounced, which would be aggressive.)

B. Remind yourself of what you want to happen as a result of the discussion, rather than waiting to see what comes up. (But remain flexible enough to respond fairly to what the other person has to say without insisting that you necessarily get it all your own way.)

C. Look him or her straight in the eye *most* of the time you are talking, rather than looking down or away. (But don't glare fixedly at him or her, for this might be responded to as aggression.)

D. Speak in a strong, steady, confident voice, avoiding gabbling, giggling, twittering, humming-and-hahing or letting the pitch of your voice rise with nervousness. (But don't shout, curse or bang your fists on the table – or on the person you are talking to.)

E. Sit or stand in a comfortable, relaxed posture, rather than looking strained and tense and ill at ease. (Don't use aggressive 'body language' like moving in close on the other person or repeatedly jabbing your finger at them. Remember, it's rude to point.)

In all the paragraphs except B above, we've been looking at assertive 'body language' (and comparing it with non-assertive body language and aggressive body language). We can do the same thing with ordinary language – verbal language – by the kind of phrases we actually use in talking with other people. Compare these examples:

First some *non-assertive* (easily ignored) remarks.

- 'Sorry to bother you, but . . . '
- 'I know I'm a nuisance . . . '
- 'It doesn't matter.'
- 'I'm sure I shouldn't be asking, but . . . '
- 'I don't mind really.'
- 'Anything you say, boss.'
- 'Would you mind very much if . . . '
- 'Well, I'm not really bothered.'

Secondly, some *aggressive* remarks that are liable to be answered equally aggressively.

- 'Look here, you . . . '
- 'You've got to be joking.'

- 'Who do you think you're talking to?'
- 'You'd better watch your step.'
- 'Why don't you start talking sense?'
- 'Just try it and see.'
- 'You've really cocked that up.'
- 'You've got no right to give my staff instructions without discussing them with me first.'

And finally, some *assertive* remarks that would stand a chance of getting the other person to be equally assertive in return, but not aggressive.

- 'What I would like is . . . '
- 'I believe that . . . '
- 'In my experience . . . '
- 'I feel that . . . '
- 'How do you feel about that?'
- 'What would you like?'
- 'Why don't we consider . . . '
- 'We have a problem.'
- 'I feel very embarrassed when you give my staff instructions without having discussed them with me.'

The Value of Repetition

You may also need to repeat your points. Some bosses are of the slippery, manipulative variety – experts at misinterpreting what you say, at apparently not hearing it, and at distracting your attention onto side-issues.

You can counter with the 'cracked record' ploy. You just keep calmly and persistently repeating the point you want to get across – e.g. 'Yes, but when will you be recommending me for promotion?' – ('Promotions are few and far between these days') – 'Yes, but when will you be recommending me for promotion?' – ('We've got quite a few promising young people coming up through the section just now') – 'Yes, but when will you be recommending me for promotion' – ('Did I tell you the trouble we're having in getting temporary staff, just now?') – 'Yes, but when will you be . . . '

Training for Assertiveness

I don't expect you to have increased your assertiveness just from reading these few paragraphs. However, I hope they've at least alerted you to the possibility that there are techniques that can be learned.

In fact, assertiveness training is quite fashionable these days. And assertiveness courses really do seem to make a difference to those who go on them – not just in managing their bosses but in dealing with all kinds of difficult people (which is to say, with most people some of the time). Why not tell your boss you'd like to go on one – without adding, 'If you don't mind, and the section can really afford it, and if it's not too much trouble.'

In the next two chapters we'll be looking at a recurring aspect of working life in which skill at boss-management (and assertiveness) becomes supremely important – performance appraisal.

Chapter 8

Preparing for Performance Appraisal

Your ability to manage your boss perhaps meets its sternest test at those times when your boss has to make an appraisal of your performance. Most organizations nowadays seem to have some sort of staff appraisal exercise at least once a year.

The well-managed ones recognize that your boss should be appraising you – and giving you helpful feedback – *continuously*, from week to week throughout the year. But they still try to ensure that, once a year, you and your boss must sit down together in order to look back over the twelve months' work *as a whole* and to plan for the *future*.

WHAT'S YOUR LOCAL SYSTEM?

Sometimes this is a very formal business. There will be piles of forms or questionnaires – forms for you to fill in, forms for your boss to fill in, forms for your boss's boss to fill in. There will be interviews – sometimes with your boss, sometimes with your boss's boss, sometimes with a specialist from Personnel. There may be special promotions panels, appeals procedures, and you will know what else besides.

In other organizations, the procedure is just as decisive in its influence on your future, but so low-key and informal that you'd hardly know it had taken place. I remember working in one organization where my boss suddenly asked me to sign 'my' section of a completed form headed 'Appraisal

Interview Report'. When I somewhat hesitantly pointed out that no-one had interviewed me yet, my boss asked me what I thought he'd been doing when he came and chatted with me over lunch in the cafeteria a few days previously!

Questions About Appraisal

So there are certain questions you need to ask yourself about the appraisal system as it works in your organization. Or, if there is no formal appraisal system, what can you do to ensure that you get regular *informal* appraisals – good ones, of course! For example:

- Do you know when you will next be appraised?
- Who will carry out the appraisal?
- What form will it take?
- Are you clear what the appraiser will be looking for?
- Will your boss encourage you to do anything to prepare for the appraisal?
- Will you be asked to contribute some kind of *self*-appraisal?
- Will you be asked to make comments or suggestions about your job or the work of the section?
- Will you be told what the appraiser (e.g. your boss) thinks about your work performance?
- Will you be given the opportunity to comment on his or her appraisal?
- Will you be involved in making any decisions that arise out of the appraisal – e.g. the possibility of a change of job?
- Will you be offered an interview with the appraiser and/or with someone more senior?
- Will you be shown and/or given a copy on any written record that results from the appraisal?

If It Isn't Offered, Ask

You may say: 'Oh no, nothing like that happens in my organization.' If so, you may want to consider how far you might want to encourage your boss to do some of it anyway.

You may, of course, feel quite satisfied with the feedback

you get from your boss day by day, and week by week. You may feel pretty confident – especially if you've been following the kind of approach discussed in previous chapters – that he or she has a good impression of you already.

On the other hand, if your boss is responsible for many staff, you may not have such regular contact. You may be somewhat uncertain as to how he or she views your work, or indeed whether he or she has any clear picture of you at all.

Either way, there is a lot to be said for persuading your boss to sit down and talk about you, at least once a year. If you've not had much opportunity so far to manage the impression you are making, then this may get you started. If your impression-management has been bubbling away all through the year, now's your chance to check out that it's been having the desired results – and to capitalize on it if possible.

WHAT MIGHT YOU GET FROM AN APPRAISAL?

There are many benefits one might get from an appraisal. Here are a few. Which of them might you find helpful?

- To check out what your boss expects of you [ ]
- To hear how your boss thinks you're doing [ ]
- To let your boss know how you think you are doing [ ]
- To get some praise for your contribution [ ]
- To present your boss with other people's comments on your performance (i.e. your sponsors/champions) [ ]
- To pinpoint difficulties that prevent you working as well as you would like to [ ]
- To discuss problems in the work of your section [ ]
- To consider new ways of doing things [ ]
- To improve working condition [ ]
- To talk about more training and/or a change of job [ ]

- To make out a case for more pay or
  responsibility   [ ]
- To discuss your readiness for promotion   [ ]
- To learn more about your boss   [ ]
✳ • To influence the way your boss sees you and
  behaves towards you in future   [ ]
- To influence what gets written about you in
  the organization's records   [ ]
- (As a last resort) To let your boss's boss
  know why you find your boss impossible to work
  for (and perhaps request a move)   [ ]
- Others (what?)   . . .

Planning Your Strategy

So, whether appraisal is something forced upon you or whether you decide to take the initiative, how can you manage it to your best advantage? There are three factors involved:

1. Doing your own self-appraisal.
2. Preparing for an appraisal interview.
3. Getting the best out of the interview.

We'll deal with the first two of these in the remainder of this chapter. We'll leave appraisal interviews until the next chapter.

By the way, in some organizations, formal appraisals are carried out by someone other than one's direct boss – though obviously in consultation with one's boss. For the sake of simplicity, in this chapter and the next, I'll talk as though all the appraising is being done by your direct boss. If things are otherwise in your organization, you can decide for yourself how you might need to adjust your strategy.

DO-IT-YOURSELF APPRAISAL

I said quite a bit in Chapter 5 about being your own appraiser throughout the year. So you shouldn't find it too difficult, once a year, to make a realistic overall appraisal of your performance. In fact, if you've honestly reflected on your work, you may be better at this than your boss is.

Anyway, don't get yourself into a situation where all you can do is respond to your boss's assessment of your performance. Make sure you've got one of your own ready – and get him or her to compare the two.

Is There a Standard Form?
What sort of points should you think about in your self-appraisal? Partly this depends on whether your appraiser (e.g. your boss) will be following some kind of standard form or questionnaire.

Your organization's appraisal form (if it has one) may contain headings such as:

- Range of duties carried out
- Quality of work
- Productivity
- Ability to meet objectives/deadlines/targets
- Accuracy
- Reliability
- Initiative/resourcefulness
- Effectiveness in dealing with people outside the organization
- Ability to cooperate with other people in section and organization
- Planning of own work
- Ability to supervise and plan work of other staff
- Effective management of resources
- Loyalty and keenness
- Interest in self-development
- Technical ability
- Communication skills
- Numerical skills
- Up-to-dateness in new approaches/technology; and so on

Some of these headings may be quite inappropriate to your

organization. Perhaps you can think of more appropriate ones that I have missed.

What is Your Boss Looking For?

The point is this: find out whether your boss will be using some standard form. If so, try to get hold of a copy of it – or at least check what headings it contains.

Also, find out how your boss is likely to be *interpreting* those headings. For instance, what might you have to do to prove your 'loyalty' or your 'interest in self-development' or your 'numerical skills'? And does your boss normally put a lot of emphasis on some headings while more or less ignoring others? Find out, if necessary by asking your boss, or colleagues who have been assessed under these headings before.

If there is no such standard form, find out whether your boss will be using headings of his or her own. Again, your boss may tell you what they are if you ask. Otherwise, colleagues who've been assessed before may be able to tell you.

What if you can't get much information about the headings under which your boss will be appraising you? Then it's up to you to decide your own headings and do your best to sell them to your boss.

This shouldn't be too difficult if you have a job description and/or a current work plan. With the help of your Work Diary, you should at least be able to make an assessment of how well you have:

(a) performed each of your main duties (which may have changed over the year);
(b) met any targets/objectives or deadlines; and
(c) exercised any responsibility you may have for staff and resources.

Produce a Self-Appraisal Report

As a result of your self-appraisal, you should be able to produce a *report* on yourself. This could be a valuable exercise even if your organization has no official appraisal procedures. It should ensure that you have at least as clear a picture of your work as your boss has – and possibly a clearer one. Ideally, it should contain plenty of EXAMPLES of your good work. If these can be backed up by written 'testimonials' (e.g. memos or letters) from satisfied colleagues or clients or customers, so much the better.

Even if your boss were never to see the contents of your self-appraisal report, producing it could still be a valuable way for you to get to grips with thoughts about what you want out of work and what you are actually getting. But, of course, you may well want to bring the contents to your boss's attention, one way or another – e.g. by discussing your self-appraisal with your boss or at least by sending him or her a copy of the report.

If it's impossible to get an appraisal interview in your organization, then sending your boss a copy of your self-appraisal may be your best way of influencing what he or she decides to put on record about you. (Especially, perhaps, if he or she has to report on you to his or her own boss.)

Nearly every boss will be interested to hear your own appraisal of your performance. Indeed, many will be pleased to find that someone (even if it's rather an interested party) has relieved them of some of the burdens of this rather tricky task. Most will prove willing to let your views influence theirs – provided you don't try to claim that your views are the only ones a sensible person could hold!

So, if you can't get an appraisal interview, your self-appraisal report may help you ensure that your boss knows what you think of yourself and what your ambitions are. But do try to press for some sort of formal discussion with your boss or you may find your points are never satisfactorily followed up.

TRY FOR A PROPER INTERVIEW

If you are going to have an interview, try to ensure that it will be a 'proper' one. Make sure the place and time is convenient to you, and that your boss has sufficient time available. You may need anything between thirty minutes and an hour of your boss's undivided attention if you are to get all your points dealt with adequately.

Don't let yourself in for being 'interviewed' on the stairs or in the car park (or, as happened to me, in the cafeteria) without any warning that you are being appraised. Such informal 'chats' are a common ploy with bosses who feel uncomfortable about appraisal. They want to be able to tell themselves (and maybe their own bosses) that they've given you an appraisal interview, but without actually getting into the embarrassing situation of having to offer some real assessment of your work – or be open to any subsequent demands for help or assistance from you.

It may also be a ploy used by manipulative bosses who are ready to put their views about you into the organization's records, but don't want to acknowledge any comment or feedback from you.

Watch out for this sort of thing. Don't let yourself get sold short. You don't want your boss to put on record appraisals that you think are unfair. Nor do you want to lose the opportunity to weigh in with some comments, suggestions and requests of your own.

If you think there is something you can get out of a formally scheduled interview with the boss – whether or not it is part of the 'official' appraisal procedures – resist any attempt to get you 'out of the way' with an impromptu chat. Tell your boss that you're sure you've got a lot of useful things to say to each other – and press him or her to agree a time when you can meet for a proper discussion. (And prepare for it as we now discuss.)

PREPARING FOR AN INTERVIEW

An interview has been defined as 'a conversation with a purpose'. In fact, it may have at least two purposes – yours and that of the other person involved. Your boss may or may not have a very clear sense of purpose. It depends how experienced he or she is in appraisal interviewing. But make sure you know what *your* purpose is.

What Do You Want?

When going into an interview, it is vital to know what you want out of it. And I do mean *you*. Many people assume that interviews are purely for the benefit of the interviewer. This is not so. You must expect to get something from the interview as well. To make sure you do, you will need to prepare – at least as well as the interviewer does.

What you might want from your interview, only you can tell. The minimum you might want out of it are:

- a clear understanding of what is expected from you in your work;
- an agreed appraisal of how you've been doing; and
- some discussions of what might be done to make your work even more productive (and satisfying) in future.

One way or another, you will need your own 'agenda' of items for discussion at the interview. To prepare for them, you will need to look back over your self-appraisal and make up a 'Wants List' to take into the interview with you.

A Preparatory Questionnaire

Some organizations offer staff a special *interview preparation questionnaire* to help you in this vital preparatory work. You may be given a copy a few days before your interview, and you will be urged to spend some time in thinking about the questions it poses. You may be invited to bring your answers to the interview – though you will usually be left to decide which of them to discuss with your interviewer.

Perhaps no such questionnaire exists in your organization. Even if it does, regard it merely as a guide. Some of its questions may seem irrelevant to your work. And there will probably be issues of your own which the questionnaire ignores but which you may want to explore further at the interview.

I've set out below some questions of the kind that might appear on an Interview Preparation Questionnaire – or which you might want to think about anyway. Even if you're not expecting to have an appraisal interview in the near future, you may still find it worthwhile considering how you would answer such questions about your work over the last few months.

In thinking about possible answers, be as specific as possible. Try to recall *examples* – easy perhaps if you have a well-kept Work Diary to refer to. For instance, in answer to Question 1(f) don't just say something general like 'staff development'. Instead, say something specific like 'Identifying staff whose jobs would be affected by new technology and arranging a variety of appropriate workshops with the equipment providers.' Notes of appreciation from satisfied staff may or may not be worth having to hand.

A SAMPLE INTERVIEW PREPARATION QUESTIONNAIRE

1. The Year's Work

(a) What have been the main duties of your job during the year, as you see them?

(b) Have these duties changed appreciably over the year?

(c) What problems (if any) have these changes caused you?

(d) What are the main standards, targets, objectives or deadlines (if any) that have been part of your job over the year?

(e) To what extent do you feel you have succeeded in meeting any such standards, targets. etc?

(f) What have you done most effectively and/or with greatest satisfaction, during the year?

(g) What have you done least effectively and/or with least satisfaction, during the year?

(h) What do you regard as your main strengths?

(i) What do you regard as your main weaknesses?

(j) What might be done to make the most of your strengths and to overcome or compensate for your weaknesses?

2. Possible Improvements

(a) Have you come across any obstacles – in your own knowledge and skills or in your job situation – that have prevented you from working as effectively, or with as much satisfaction, as you would have wished?

(b) If so, how might they be overcome or avoided?

(c) Is there any way your job might be changed – both to your benefit and to that of the section – so as to enable you to spend a greater percentage of your time on the kinds of work you do most effectively and with most satisfaction?

(d) Is there any aspect of your work in which you might feel that your boss should be providing more guidance or support?

(e) Is there any aspect of your work in which you think you might benefit from further training? If so, do you know where such training is to be obtained?

(f) If you were in charge of your section's work, what changes would you like to see made to the way things are done?

3. The Year Ahead

(a) What duties do you expect to be performing in the year ahead?

(b) What objectives/goals/deadlines/targets do you expect you will have to reach?

(c) What additional resources, support or training do you think might be needed?

(d) In order to increase both your productivity and your job satisfaction in the coming year, what additional things might need to be done by:

- yourself?
- your boss?
- other managers?
- other staff?
- anyone else?

(e) If the improvements in (c) and (d) were made, what might you expect to achieve in the coming twelve months that you were unable to achieve over the last year?

---

4. General Issues

Are there any other issues you would like to discuss - concerning, for example:

(a) Your present job?
(b) Your individual interests and abilities – particularly any that are not fully used in your present job?
(c) Your ambitions, e.g to move on to other jobs in the organization?
(d) Prospects for further training or self-development?
(e) Anything else?

Unless you really are about to go into an appraisal interview, you won't have spent very much time considering the above questions. But you may find it worth coming back to them – and spending an hour or more with them – next time you do face such an interview. Remember, the way to manage your performance appraisal is to be at least as well prepared as your boss.

In fact, answers to questions like these are worth keeping in mind throughout the year. You never know when an ordinary chat with the boss is likely to take on some of the overtones of an appraisal interview!

DECIDE ON YOUR GOALS

As I said earlier, it's essential to know what you want from an interview. If you've had a chance to prepare properly, you should know what *goals* you will be trying to achieve. Your boss will also have goals – and you may have some in common. But the discussion will be pointless, as far as you are concerned, unless you are pursuing some clearly-defined goals of your own.

Varieties of Goal

You may be merely seeking a bit of appreciation for a job well done or you may be looking for a new set of duties you believe you might do better. You may be hoping to get some kind of additional support from your boss in 'payment' for all the excellent support you've given him or her. You may want a bigger salary, or a new job title, or more control over policy and resources.

You may be seeking to defuse your boss's concern about what he or she may see as your shortcomings. Perhaps you'll be out to demonstrate that you've clearly overcome them since you were last assessed. Or maybe you'll be aiming to show that they are a result of faults in the system (not in you) and that your boss can help overcome them by providing certain kinds of support.

You may also have a number of relatively trivial goals – more office space, a cordless telephone, a desk chair that doesn't send you home every evening with your spine in knots. These and many other benefits you may be able to argue for on the grounds that they will improve your efficiency and therefore that of the section. And thus you will be able to provide your boss with even better support.

What are your Priorities?

What may be more difficult is deciding what is the *minimum* you will settle for. If, for instance, you're really after a completely new set of duties (or a new boss), might you agree to make do with modifications to your existing job? Or with additional training to help you do it more effectively and with greater satisfaction? Or might you be content simply with some long-overdue assurances that you are doing the present job perfectly adequately? This all needs to be thought about *before* the interview.

As in any negotiation, you will be unlikely to get everything on your list. Once you start discussions with your boss, you'll need to concentrate most of your fire on the major targets. Don't, for example, let your boss side-track you into debating which particular form of chair you'd like, only to find there

is no time left to discuss the new duties you'd like to take on.
Keep an eye on your priorities.

The Bottom Line
At the very least, you need to decide:

(a) What you would *ideally* like to see HAPPEN as a result
of the appraisal interview.
(b) What's the *best* you think likely to happen.
(c) What's the *least* you would feel ready to settle for.

PSYCHING YOURSELF UP

A vital part of preparing for your interview is to get yourself into the right frame of mind. How do you normally feel
when you go into an appraisal interview? If you haven't yet
had such an interview, how would you expect to feel? Here
are some reactions that different people have given to this
question:

A. 'Worried to death about which of my "failings" the boss
might want to throw at me.'
B. 'Apprehensive, in case my boss just isn't "on my wave-
length".'
C. 'Keyed up, but with nothing really to be anxious about.'
D. 'No feelings – it's just another pointless annual ritual.'
E. 'Determined to work for the outcomes I want from the
interview.'
F. 'Confident that I know what the results will be.'

Are any of these attitudes similar to yours? Clearly, some
of them are more positive than others. As a results, the
individual is likely to be properly psyched up to get something worthwhile from the interview. For example, A and
B both sound like people who are resigned to things just
happening to them – in a way that is beyond their control.
D seems too cynical to expect much (or get much) from the

event. F is either cynical or fatalistic – believing that whatever might come from the interview (if anything) is already decided – or else is perhaps a shade over-confident about the way these things can turn out.

On the whole, C's is quite a useful frame of mind to be in, if you can manage it. More important, however, is to have the sort of attitude expressed by E – who is concentrating on what she or he wants to get out of the interview (regardless of what may happen along the way).

Why Some People Get Nervous
All the same, many people do get very apprehensive, if not downright paranoid, about interviews with their boss. This is not surprising, especially if they are not used to talking at any length with the boss, day by day. They may not know enough about their boss (see Chapter 3) to be able to predict how he or she will be.

Besides which, they may be all too aware that their strengths and weaknesses will be up for discussion. While most of us are quite happy to natter at length about our strengths, we aren't usually quite as ready to do the same for our weaknesses – not unless we have a lot of trust in the person we are discussing them with. The thought of other people's criticisms (even if, perhaps especially if, they are justified) can seem very threatening – particularly when those people have power over us. And bosses, by definition, are people who have power over us.

Why You Should be Confident
However, there should really be no need for *you* to be anxious about an appraisal interview – not if you are putting into practice the ideas we are discussing in this book. There are four main reasons why you should be able to approach such an interview with confidence:

1. You will expect the interview to be *productive*. You will not approach it as a contest between you and your boss. Neither you nor your boss (I hope) will see

it as an eyeball-to-eyeball confrontation or a ruthless cross-examination intended to make you feel stupid and incompetent.

Instead, if you have been managing your boss reasonably well hitherto, you should be able to approach it as a joint planning session. It may, in fact, be rather similar to many other such discussions you have had during the year – except this time you may be planning what needs to be done over the next year or more, rather than just the next few days or weeks.

2. If you have taken pains to 'know' your boss, you will be able to *anticipate* what line he or she is likely to take in the interview. If your boss is anything like a proper manager, his or her chief concern will not be to find fault or pass judgement, let alone to give you a rollocking.

For your boss, the appraisal interview is part of *managing* – achieving results through other people (you, in this case). He or she is not going to get anything achieved for the section by making you feel bad about yourself.

The wise boss will be most concerned with how to make the most of your strengths – and will dwell on a weakness only if he or she sees some prospect of helping you overcome it. Does this sound like the boss you've learned to know (if not love)? Do you have any doubts about your boss's ability to act like a manager in this situation – rather than like counsel for the prosecution? If you do, then don't just sit back and settle for whatever he or she throws at you. Make it clear to your boss – in the most tactful way possible, of course – that you are looking to him or her for practical help and guidance (rather than for unconstructive criticism).

Maybe your boss will also be wondering what you are going to try to get him or her to do for you. And perhaps he or she will be wondering what extra effort or support he or she can get from you in return for it.

3. You will have done your *'homework'*. You have prepared for the interview at least as well as your boss has. You may have been keeping a Work Diary for several months. You will certainly have given considerable thought to preparing for the interview. And you will *know* yourself – your strengths and your weaknesses, the objectives or targets you have achieved and those you are less happy about.

   So you should have a pretty good idea of the kinds of issue your boss might want to discuss with you. You may even be able to 'rehearse' parts of the interview in your mind – by imagining what you would say to someone like you if *you* were the boss, and how you might respond.

4. Above all, you will have some *goals* of your own to achieve. As I said earlier, the appraisal interview is a formal opportunity for you to get the boss to consider changes *you* would like to see made – new duties or additional responsibilities, new facilities, more training, or whatever.

   It is also your opportunity to correct any mistaken notions your boss may have about what you do, how well you do it, and why. And, not least, it gives you an excellent opportunity to remind your boss of how much he or she depends on your support – and of what he or she needs to do to ensure it continues and grows in strength.

☆   ☆   ☆

In Chapter 9 we'll consider how to manage the interview itself.

Chapter 9

Making the Most of an Appraisal Interview

Remember that an appraisal interview is not just for your boss's benefit. There's plenty you can expect to get out of it too. Some such more or less formal discussion with your boss may be the only chance you get to let her or him know what you need in order to further your career. And if you don't bring your career needs to your boss's attention, the odds are that no-one else will.

WHAT'S TO BE GAINED?

Some people moan about appraisal interviews and reckon they never get anything from them. They say things like: 'She didn't even seem to know who I was' or 'I was hoping we'd talk about giving me more responsibility – but he never went near the subject.'

This sort of frustration is usually the lot of people who either:

(a) haven't prepared thoroughly for the interview; or
(b) don't play an active part in it.

It's important to realize that an appraisal interview, or any other serious discussion with the boss, need not be something that just 'happens' to you. To a greater or lesser extent, it can be what you *make* it.

One might say: Don't just go to it – go *for* it! And: Don't just sit there – *do* something!

GOING FOR IT

To get the most from an appraisal interview, you have to be in the right frame of mind. As we discussed in Chapter 8, you may need to psych yourself up. I mentioned several reasons why you should be able to go into your interview with confidence – not least the fact that you have a set of *goals* (your 'Wants List') that you hope to attain.

All the same, you won't be unusual if you also feel a certain amount of anxiety or apprehension – even if it's only about whether you'll get what you are after. Indeed, you need to be at least a little 'keyed up' if you're to make the most of any sort of meeting, whether it involves your being appraised or not. Otherwise, you just wouldn't be 'on the ball'.

You might also bear in mind that your boss may be apprehensive too. She or he may be anxious about whether you are going to be making demands that she or he will find difficult to satisfy. Remember, your boss is 'piggy in the middle' between your expectations and the limitations that her or his own bosses try to impose.

She or he may also be wondering how to talk about ways in which you might become more productive – but without seeming to criticize you for being less productive in the past. This isn't always easy – even for interviewers who have done it before. And your boss will have no more experience of interviewing you than you have of being interviewed by her or him!

THE TIMING AND SHAPE OF AN INTERVIEW

An interview is not like an ordinary discussion or a conversation. These usually just happen when they happen, go on for

as long as seems worthwhile, and have no particular shape
one can predict in advance. But with an interview, it's always
worth thinking, before you get started, about both its timing
and its shape.

The Timing of an Interview

How long will an appraisal interview last? Before you start
your discussion with your boss, make a point of checking
just how much time she or he is allowing for it. You may
feel you need at least thirty minutes, maybe a full hour. If the
time your boss is proposing seems inadequate for what you
want to accomplish, suggest that you both might benefit by
postponing the interview until there is more time available.

Likewise, if your boss starts taking telephone calls or chat-
ting to people who just happen to drop in once you have
begun your discussion. Sympathetically point out that you
can see this is not a very convenient time for her or him,
and suggest you meet again later – or move to a room where
there will be no telephone or other callers. For you both to get
something of value from the discussion, you need to be able
to concentrate exclusively on what one another has to say.

Three Essentials

So, there are three things to aim at as far as timing is
concerned:

1. Try to get the interview arranged for a day and time that
   is convenient to *you*. Whatever happens, don't let yourself get drawn into what looks like being an appraisal
   interview without prior notice – and before you've had
   time to think out your strategy. If your boss comes at
   you out of the blue, mention some urgent business that
   you must attend to and ask for a properly scheduled
   interview.
2. Find out, in advance, just how much time your boss is
   planning to make available for you. And, if you feel this
   is inadequate, ask for longer – if necessary backing up
   your request by mentioning some of the areas you'd like

to discuss. (But be careful not to give too much away that might forewarn your boss and allow her or him to anticipate what line you'll be taking and to prepare counter-arguments.)

3. Once the interview has started, don't allow yourself to be rushed. Or you may end up like the many patients who leave a doctor's surgery saying 'It was all over before I got to my main point.' If your boss is handling things properly, she or he will have done all that is possible to avoid interruptions. If the interruptions start coming, or your boss starts hogging the conversation, suggest that you might both benefit from beginning again on another day.

Shaping the Interview

To make the most of whatever time is available, the interview needs to follow some kind of shape or pattern. Who decides what the shape of the interview will be? Remember that the interview belongs to you as well as to your boss. So the shape should, ideally, be one that is agreeable to you as well as to your boss.

All the same, many bosses will have quite fixed ideas about shaping up the interview. They, after all, are probably doing several interviews – whereas this is your one and only. So they may unthinkingly apply to you the same pattern they have got into the habit of using with everyone else.

A Possible Pattern

One pattern that many bosses will more or less follow goes like this:

A. Introduction

1. A bit of social chat to 'break the ice' and put you (and maybe your boss) at your ease.
2. Agree/explain the purpose of the interview.
3. State the benefits likely to be gained by both parties.

4. Remind you perhaps of what you agreed in your last appraisal interview (if anything).
5. Encourage you to refer to whatever notes you made as part of your interview preparation (Chapter 8).
6. Ask you to mention the main areas you want to discuss.
7. Agree the 'agenda' for the interview by merging what you want to discuss with what your boss wants to discuss.

B. Main body of the interview

1. Ask you about your job – as set out in your job description/work plan (and/or as it has evolved since you and the boss last took an overall look at it) – your main duties, objectives and targets, problems and opportunities, satisfactions and dislikes.
2. Review what you have achieved, giving especial credit for areas of development and improvement.
3. Explore any areas where you and/or your boss feel you have achieved less than you might have done – sharing ideas as to what factors might account for this.
4. Ask about your ideas for changes that might improve your productivity and work satisfaction and/or that of the section.
5. Review your long-term career plans and ambitions.
6. In the light of 5, consider what you might be doing over the next, say, twelve months.
7. Agree your job description for the coming year, together with any objectives, targets, etc.
8. Agree what needs to be done or provided by you, by your boss, and maybe by others – e.g. new responsibilities or duties, promotion, training, new facilities, change of policy or procedures, and so on.

C. Conclusion

1. Summarize the main points covered in the interview.
2. Summarize what you have agreed to do.
3. Summarize what your boss has agreed to do (or get others to do).

4. Agree on how to keep each other informed about progress on what you have both agreed to do and changes you have agreed should be made.

Influencing the Pattern

How far do you think a pattern like that above might suit your purposes? It would probably allow you to raise all the issues you may have thought about in working through the interview preparation questionnaire (Chapter 8). If you foresee any difficulty about getting all your points in, tell your boss how you would like to see the pattern amended.

What if your boss shows no sign of having given any thought to the shape of the interview? In that case, you might want to suggest something like the one above. Or you might suggest you work through the headings in sections 1–4 of your interview preparation questionnaire – or through any 'official' preparation form if your organization issues one.

Yet another line might be to ask your boss to respond to your Self Appraisal Report if you sent her or him a copy before the interview. Whatever you may have in mind as your own ideal 'agenda', take a copy along with you, just in case your boss seems willing to go with it.

Anyway, both you and your boss should be agreed on the shape of the interview before you start getting into the main issues.

Staying Flexible

Expect your interview to follow a pattern. But don't worry if it doesn't stick to it rigidly. Your discussion may leap ahead to points later in the 'agenda', and also back-track to earlier ones. This is all right so long as you're confident that all your points are being dealt with. You can then afford to stay flexible.

You need worry only if your interview seems to be drifting or getting bogged down in trivialities. It may then be up to you to suggest a return to the agreed 'agenda'. Don't forget that your boss may sometimes have less experience of interviewing than you have of being interviewed. So be prepared to take the lead from time to time.

Make Notes
Take a writing pad to your interview and be prepared to make notes. A lot can be said in an appraisal interview – but much may be forgotten (or misremembered) unless the main points are jotted down as you go along.

Make a special note of aspects of your work that your boss praises or finds fault with. Note also any suggestions your boss makes about how you might improve or develop your work in the future, and any additional help or resources she or he promises to provide for you.

Such notes may be very important if your boss is one of those who are liable to 'move the goalposts' later on, or deny that certain promises were ever made. Your boss may not be too comfortable about your making notes. But she or he will probably be making notes, so why shouldn't you? After all – as you may reassure you boss – you expect to be getting a lot of valuable ideas from her or him during this session and you wouldn't want to risk forgetting any of them, would you?

HANDLING THE DISCUSSION

Now let's think about how to get maximum benefit from the discussion and attain your goals. There are perhaps three main aspects to concern yourself with:
  – presenting the points you want to make;
  – paying close attention to your boss; and
  – dealing with criticism.

Presenting your Points
The interview is your opportunity to let your boss know what you think about your present job and your future – and to make clear what extra support or resources you would like in order to become even more indispensable to your boss.

You should have plenty of time to present your ideas. Ideally, your boss should be prepared to let you do most of the talking – perhaps you should expect to be able to speak for about two-thirds of the time available.

Make sure you don't let this go to your head. Remember the points you want to make, and stick to them. Refer to whatever notes you made while working through your interview preparation questionnaire.

Don't ramble all over the place. Resist the temptation to wander (or get drawn) into side-issues. Don't waste this precious opportunity by getting irrelevant.

Remember that the appraisal interview is something of a set piece in the game of 'impression management'. At the same time, show proper respect for your boss in what you say. For instance, you'll know better than to tell outright lies about the job or how you perform it. But which of the following have you been tempted into during such interviews in the past? (Don't tick any if it's too painful to remember.)

- Exaggerations [ ]
- Ignoring awkward questions [ ]
- Pretending ignorance [ ]
- Blinding the boss with jargon [ ]
- Pooh-poohing your boss's concerns [ ]
- Blaming everyone but yourself [ ]

No doubt we've all been tempted into such desperate measures on occasion. But they don't do us any good. If we evade the issue, or try to flannel or blind the boss with technical details, or slander people who aren't there to defend themselves, we'll be suggesting that the boss is too dim to see what we're up to. Most bosses will take exception to this. Since we're not showing respect for them, they'll lose their respect for us.

Discussing successes and failures.
So, play it straight. Be self-assured and assertive, without

being aggressive. Focus on your achievements and improvements, but don't suggest they're due to your being a superior sort of person. (Although you shouldn't, of course, hinder your boss from coming to that conclusion for him/herself!)

Concentrate on describing the job that was well done and how you felt about it, rather than on how clever you think you are. Mention any tributes you've received from people known to, and respected by, your boss – but only if you can do so without seeming to be crowing. Give proper credit to any circumstances that have favoured you or to other people who have helped you succeed. Show that you are proud of your achievements, but without being arrogant.

Leave room for your boss to get in with one or two congratulatory remarks of her or his own. And accept them gracefully but as no more than your due. This is no time for self-deprecating remarks like 'It was nothing, really' or 'Anyone could have done it.'

If you must admit to mistakes and failures, try to seem equally forthcoming. But aim to turn them to your advantage. Try to show that you have learned something from them. Most bosses will agree that a failure is often not entirely a bad thing if it has taught you a lesson – one that will help you avoid that kind of failure in future.

For instance, here are various statements describing successes and failures. How do you feel these might go down with the boss, in the light of the comments I've made above?

1. 'Some of us have been very encouraged by the comments we've had about our marketing proposals since we went on that course last May.'
2. 'Everyone in the section comes to me for comments on their marketing proposals. I guess they remember how my ideas were considered outstanding on that course.'
3. 'I know we lost a lot of time and money on that project; but how am I supposed to keep things running smoothly when other sections don't send me up-to-date information?'
4. 'After that cock-up I had with Personnel, I'll know

better than to assume other sections follow the same procedures as we do in ours.'

The first statement and the last seem to follow the 'rules' I suggested above. (Statement 1 leaves room for your boss to recall how outstanding your particular marketing proposals were; while Statement 4 invites comments about differences between sections rather than about your ignorance of them.) Statement Number 2, however, sounds arrogant, and number 3 is evasive. As such, 2 would be liable to irritate your boss and the question in 3 might get rather an abrasive answer.

Paying Close Attention

As well as telling your boss everything you want her or him to know, you must also be prepared to listen and to watch.

Clearly, you can't just go nattering on with no regard for your boss. At the very least, you need to be sensitive to how she or he is receiving your remarks. This means you must listen carefully to any comments or questions that are put to you – and to any unexpected, and perhaps embarrassing, silences. And you must watch your boss's *physical gestures* also.

Take that last point first. 'Body language' it is sometimes called. You can tell a lot about how your talk is being received from the way the interviewer uses her or his body.

Body language

For instance, a slow nodding of the head may indicate that your boss is interested in what you are saying. But a rapid nodding often means 'Yes, yes, yes, do get on with it for goodness' sake.' You could be even more sure of agreement if the interviewer began leaning forward in her or his seat. But if she or he were sitting well back, especially with arms folded, it might indicate that your ideas were being rejected.

Such gestures may give you a clue as to whether you can go on with what you are saying or whether you should change tack. But the signals you get are often unclear or ambiguous. For instance, imagine you are having an interview with *your* boss. Which the following do you think might indicate that what you are saying is perhaps not having the desired effect? Your boss begins to:

- fiddle with papers
- make notes
- doodle
- glance frequently at the clock
- stare out of the window
- frown
- pace around the room

Almost all of these bits of body language might mean your boss was beginning to get bored, irritated or impatient. But, to 'make notes' could be a compliment to the importance of what you are saying. And if your boss started to 'pace around the room' it might be intended purely to relieve a sudden cramp. It's up to you – there, in the situation – to watch out for such movements, and decide whether they have something to tell you. And, if so, what it is. The better you know your boss (Chapter 3), the more confidently you'll be able to interpret her or his reactions.

Keep a watch too on your own body language. What messages is your body giving – often without your knowledge – to your boss? For example:

- Don't offer a flabby handshake – taken by many people, whether rightly or wrongly, to reveal a drippy personality – but don't attempt a bone-crusher (likely to be thought aggressive) instead.
- Look your interviewer firmly in the eye when you meet, and keep up plenty of 'eye contact' throughout.
- Don't slouch in your chair (or put your feet up on the desk) – but don't sit nervously on the edge of your seat either.
- Look alert and energetic (which is what you should be feeling also – after all, you've got goals to attain).

- If you are a smoker, refrain unless your interviewer smokes and invites you to.
- Control your voice.

Control your voice.
When people are a bit nervous, their voices often become rather high-pitched and thin, or even squeaky. The person concerned may not notice this, but listeners will. At the very least they will think the person is nervous or anxious. At worst, the listener – a boss, for example – may, without consciously thinking about it, take the person less seriously than if she or he were speaking with a deeper, more resonant voice. Such a voice is generally held to give the speaker 'bottom' – and makes that person someone whose opinions are likely to be weightier than those of people with lighter voices. (This is just one reason among the many why women are so often at a disadvantage in discussions with men.)

Both Margaret Thatcher and Neil Kinnock suffered this problem during their early days in front-line politics, and both had to learn to lower the pitch of their voices on public occasions. Consider whether you might need to do likewise in an appraisal interview (and elsewhere). Don't gabble either – speak at a measured pace, and don't be afraid to pause now and again.

What's your boss saying?
So much for watching your boss's body language and your own – and controlling your own voice. Now what about listening to your boss's voice? If you are to know what is going on in your boss's mind, you will need to keep alert to her or his comments and questions. Even if you have two-thirds of the conversation, it must *relate* to your boss's one-third. For instance:

- If your boss makes a comment or asks a question you don't understand, ask for it to be explained. Bosses aren't necessarily any better than the rest of us at making themselves clear. Don't fear you will be considered thick if you have to say 'What exactly are you getting at, there?' Your boss is more likely to consider you thick if you just ignore the point or address yourself to some different point instead.

- If you understand the comment or question, but don't know the answer, admit it. Don't do what so many politicians do, and answer a question that has not been asked. Don't try to flannel your boss (unless, of course, you've already had a lot of successful experience of doing so).

- Don't take all comments and questions to mean exactly what they say. For example, 'Tell me what you've been doing this year' isn't really an invitation to give a page-by-page reading from your Work Diary.

- Even if your boss does seem to mean it – e.g. 'How do you manage to work with old Scroggins,' have a care. You may decide that total frankness might not be in your best interests.

- Look out for assumptions, beliefs or prejudices that may lie *beneath* your boss's statements or questions. (The most famous example of this sort of question is 'Have you stopped beating your wife?')

Underlying beliefs and assumptions.
As another example of the last point, what belief might you think lay beneath the following remark, if it were made to you by your boss?: 'Well, at least we can't accuse you of poor relations with the suppliers, this year.' And how might you respond to it?

The boss seems to be implying that you could have been accused of poor relations with the suppliers in at least one previous year. Do you let this pass, or do you respond to it? If you don't agree that the accusation would have been fair in some previous year, then you will no doubt want to challenge it. Otherwise, it may influence the way your boss sees you now and in future. Ask your boss exactly what she or he means by the statement, and what past events she or he is thinking of.

Here is another question that may have something behind it: 'Are you thinking of starting a family soon?'

What might be the idea behind this one? The boss may well be assuming that the interviewee will shortly be less useful to the section if she is thinking of starting a family. I say 'she' because it is unlikely that such a question would be addressed to a man. A still common underlying assumption, then, is that once a couple have children, it will be the woman's rôle to look after them. It will be her career, not the man's, that gets interrupted or ended altogether. This may be an untrue assumption, because the couple may have decided to share the child-rearing. Such half-hidden assumptions can work against you unless you get them out into the open where they can be discussed and perhaps destroyed.

Most organizations that claim to be Equal Opportunity Employers would, of course, disown such a question as sexist. It implies that women can be expected to act differently from men, simply because they are women, rather than taking their individual decisions and choices into account.

Such a sexist attitude would be discouraged by an Equal Opportunity Employer. Managers should have been told to treat people individually on their merits. So bosses should have been asked not to assume that a particular person will or will not be able to do such-and-such merely because she or he is a woman/man or black or partially disabled, and so on. Each individual should be given an equal opportunity, without prejudice, to reveal and develop her or his talents. All of which sounds fine from the organization's point of view, but individual bosses are still liable to let their prejudices slip into the discussion.

Forms of prejudice.

Prejudice can take many forms. On the one hand, it may mean that you are simply not taken as seriously as you think you should be. On the other hand, it may mean you are kept out of jobs that you could handle as well as anyone. Have you ever felt *unfairly* treated in your working life, whether in an appraisal or elsewhere, on account of your:

- Race   [ ]
- Religion   [ ]
- Politics   [ ]
- Sex   [ ]
- Sexual habits   [ ]
- Age   [ ]
- Style of dress   [ ]
- Present grade   [ ]
- Length of time in the organization   [ ]
- Country of birth   [ ]
- Regional accent   [ ]
- Physical handicap   [ ]
- Personality clash   [ ]
- Others (what?)   . . .

I hope you will not run into such prejudice in your appraisal
interviews. But you should know your boss well enough to
be able to anticipate whether anything of this sort is likely
to arise.

'Personal' questions or statements don't necessarily indicate prejudice. But they may do. So watch out for it. If
it becomes more than you feel you could deal with, don't
get drawn into a hot dispute. Don't let your boss see that
you are discomforted. Merely indicate that you find such
remarks inappropriate and, if necessary, consider suggesting
that you would prefer to have your interview with someone
else – perhaps with your boss's boss.

Dealing with Criticism

Prejudice is one thing, and not to be tolerated. Criticism is
quite another, and one that we all have to put up with. None
of us is perfect, and all of us have areas in which we could
improve. Unavoidably, an appraisal interview is an occasion
when we are likely to be reminded of some of our less than
perfect qualities.

Knowing what you do of your boss, for what purpose might
you expect her or him to make any criticisms of your performance in an appraisal interview?

- To make you feel guilty [ ]
- To help you overcome your weaknesses [ ]
- To give you a chance to explain [ ]
- To identify ways of improving the job [ ]
- To show what high standards your boss has [ ]
- To allow your boss to let off steam [ ]
- Others (what?) . . .

Ask for constructive criticism.
You know best what your own boss is likely to be up to. The most productive reasons she or he might have for criticism would be to give you a chance to explain any weak areas in your performance and to look for ways of helping you change, or changing the job situation, in order to help overcome such weaknesses.

You won't have too much respect for a boss who is merely trying to make you feel guilty or just letting off steam. Nor should she or he be criticizing aspects of your personality that you can do nothing about.

Any criticisms should be limited to abilities and aspects of performance that are *within your power to improve* – provided you get the right kind of support or additional resources or training. In short, if you are to be criticized, you have a right to expect criticism that is *sympathetic* and *constructive*.

Ways of coping with criticism.
Here are some suggestions to bear in mind when facing criticism, whether in appraisal interviews or at other times. Only you can decide which of the suggestions might work with your particular boss.

1. Listen as coolly as you can – without interrupting.
2. Establish exactly what it is that's being criticized. Don't accept vague generalities, e.g. 'It's your whole attitude that's wrong.' Ask politely for some specific examples. Expect your boss to say something like: 'Well take last Monday afternoon when I asked you to . . .'

3. Try to be objective. Is your boss's criticism one you might have made yourself (perhaps while considering your interview preparation questionnaire)? If not, can you see the truth of it now that your boss has made it?

4. If you think the criticism unfair or based on faulty evidence, don't try to simply dismiss it out of hand. To do so is, in effect, to criticize your boss for getting it wrong. Besides annoying her or him, it would simply get you into a sterile exchange of the 'No, I don't' – 'Yes you do' variety.

   A more productive ploy is to remind your boss of *contradictory* evidence or examples – e.g. 'Would you have said that of me last month, when you complimented me on the good reports you'd had about me from . . .?' (This is the sort of situation where you get a real pay-off from having kept a Work Diary.)

5. Don't attack your boss for being stupid, prejudiced or having a short memory (even if you believe it). Try to remain calm and dignified. You need to keep your wits about you.

6. Don't be apologetic about faults which are not in your immediate power to overcome; and don't offer excuses or suggest the fault doesn't matter. Be frank about it – e.g. 'Yes, I agree. I can quite see that I'm weak in the area of . . .'

   But, where appropriate, do explain the circumstances in which the fault shows itself – e.g. 'I know I tend to do that in cases where I can't see the difference between . . .'

7. Ask your boss what she or he thinks can be done about your faults or shortcomings. This is the acid test of whether your boss is just letting off steam or has really given some thought to helping you improve your work performance. Try to have some ideas of your own also – especially if you don't much reckon those (if any) that your boss is putting forward.

8. Invite even more criticism – e.g. 'Yes, I see that my report writing could be improved. Is there anything

else you would like to see me improve at?' Exhaust your boss's capacity to criticize. Get it all out in the open now, rather than leaving it to fester in his or her mind.

Impress your boss with your willingness to listen and to learn from her or his assessments of you. (Actually, the more you invite criticism, the more you may find that your boss is finding *positive* things to say about you. Do you think this would be likely with your boss?)

9. Don't let the appraisal of your job performance end on your weaknesses. Work the discussion round to your strengths. In what ways are you doing your work satisfactorily? In which areas does the boss particularly value your support? How might she or he like to see these strengths made more use of?

GOING FOR YOUR GOALS

Throughout the interview, you need to be asking yourself: 'Am I getting what I wanted from this interview?' Think back to your interview preparation and the *goals* you decided on.

Have you had the kind of feedback you were looking for from your boss? Have you had a satisfactory discussion of how to overcome any weaknesses and how to make the best possible use of your strengths?

Have you made clear to your boss what you need in order to help you do an even better job in future – and be even more supportive and indispensable? Check through the items on your 'Wants List'. For how many of them have you got your boss's agreement?

Try not to suggest that you are asking for treats or indulgences – rewards for being good. Don't emphasize how much you will get out of them. Your aim should be to show how each item on your list (whether a salary increase or a more comfortable chair) will ultimately benefit your boss. They will better enable you to help meet her or his goals.

Persistence and Realism

Be persistent in asking for what you want, but be realistic. You probably won't get everything you're asking for. (Not unless your boss is desperate to keep you and has somehow got wind that you are being head-hunted or are applying for jobs elsewhere!)

But regard an initial NO as a possible MAYBE and a MAYBE as a probable YES. Of course, the less you need the job and the more your boss knows that she or he needs you, the more you can pile on the pressure. The immortal phrase 'I'm beginning to wonder if there's really a future for me in this section/organization' can even be heard to fall, more in sorrow than in anger, from your lips.

Your boss may try to fob you off with parent-like platitudes – e.g. 'We'll just have to wait and see' or 'Things are a bit tight at present' or 'I can't make a decision like that without consulting X or Y (mummy/daddy).' Don't be put off too easily. If you judge that she or he is simply stalling you, ask for a definite (near) date by which your request will be reviewed. Check out exactly what sort of tightness it is that makes such worthwhile needs so difficult to meet and just what will have to happen to ease that tightness. If you judge it necessary, suggest that you discuss your needs with a higher authority, e.g. your boss's boss or even higher (with or without your boss present).

Obviously, how far you care to push all this depends on your judgement as to how far it is likely to bring you more good than harm. You don't want to make an enemy of your boss. Calling her or his bluff is one thing (assuming your boss would prefer to concede to you as little as possible in return for as much support as you're capable of giving) – but you don't want to back your boss into a corner where she or he feels resentful or risks losing face with higher authority. She or he might then be looking for an opportunity to get even.

All this is a delicate balancing act. Performing it well depends on knowing what you are worth, knowing your boss's goals and ways of dealing with people, and knowing the culture of your organization and what it can do for the staff it values.

But perhaps you think this all sounds like pie in the sky. You may be saying: 'I'd be lucky to get out of an appraisal interview with my skin in one piece, never mind clutching a bag of goodies.'

You may be right, unless you've been assiduously applying the techniques of boss-management over several months preceding the interview. The interview is merely the tip of the iceberg. It is most unlikely that anything you might do there could radically change a negative impression your boss has formed of you over the months preceding it. So, in order to be in the best possible bargaining position at your next performance appraisal or review, start managing your boss today!

WHEN THE INTERVIEW IS OVER

Eventually, you and your boss will have said all there is to say, or all that time allows. You will, we hope, have had a satisfactory discussion about your job and your performance and what you might be doing in the future – both to improve on any weaknesses you may have and build on your strengths. You will have done your best to convince your boss that she or he can regard you as increasingly indispensable and that several 'wants' you have mentioned will be worth providing you with because they will enable you to give your boss even more effective support – perhaps even by taking on new duties and responsibilities.

You will have agreed to do certain things in the future, and so will your boss. She or he may also have made promises on behalf of other people – trainers, other managers, personnel staff, or whoever. It is as well to *compare notes* on main points of agreement before concluding the interview.

As soon as possible after the interview, make sure that your boss sends you a memo (or you send your boss one) confirming what was agreed between you. If promises don't start materializing as and when you agreed, chase them up.

And get on with working as successfully as you can, and being seen to do so – and aim to make even more of your *next* appraisal interview.

Chapter 10

When the Boss is Impossible

For all I know, most bosses are reasonably decent people, no less rational and well-meaning than the rest of us. They are different from us, however. They have power over us. And their interests are different too. They are responsible not just for their own individual work, as we all are, but also for the work of a whole team or section. They have to see that the section's task gets done.

So, as I have been at pains to point out in this book, even the best of bosses needs managing. Otherwise, you may find that the task gets done to your boss's satisfaction, but your needs get overlooked in the process.

And that's just the basically decent, well-meaning bosses. There are others – which may or may not be why you are reading this book. With these you need to take a particularly firm hand or you may end up not simply overlooked but trampled into the ground.

ARE BAD BOSSES BORN OR MADE?

Why are some bosses more difficult to deal with than others? As I suggested in the first chapter, the reasons are probably a combination of one or more of the following factors:

- something to do with the organization;
- something to do with the personality of the boss;
- something to do with you (and your colleagues) and how you behave towards the boss.

You'll already have thought about the factors that make your boss what she or he is. Sometimes, one factor alone is enough to make a boss difficult to live with:

- A bureaucratic, rule-driven organization can grind down the most creative of bosses and drive him or her into going 'by the book' like everyone else.
- Sometimes a thoroughgoing bully or blockhead or blowhard can get into a position of power and survive for long enough to do quite a bit of damage in an organization that wouldn't, on the face of things, seem to be such a person's natural stamping ground.
- And, of course, it's just possible that you have a way with you that makes a monster out of some manager that everyone else gets on with perfectly well. (Though not after reading this book, of course!)

So, when you get a boss who seems unusually troublesome, don't automatically put it down to 'personality'. He or she may not even be 'going through a phase', e.g. the so-called mid-life crisis.

The cause of your boss's apparent awkwardness may lie in something the organization is doing to him or her. Try to find out if this is the case, and if possible, offer what help you can. Or the trouble may lie in something you and/or your colleagues have done (or not done). Again, try to find out and take action to improve the way your boss feels about it.

DEALING WITH THE IMPOSSIBLE BOSS

Despite my remarks above, we still have to recognize that some bosses are likely to prove strangely resistant to the management approaches we have been discussing in this book.

Despite all your efforts, they remain less than satisfactory. In fact, they may be a positive threat to you. They may, for instance:

- Be so incompetent that your own work is jeopardized.

- Be scornful and derisory about your work.
- Actively try to undermine your standing in the section or organization.
- Keep threatening you (unjustly) with disciplinary proceedings.
- Cheat the organization or its clients/customers and expect you to go along with it.
- Unmistakably favour some colleagues (e.g. a mistress or lover) at the expense of more deserving staff.
- Take all the credit for your best work and give you no reward in return.
- Fly off the handle and shout and scream at you in response to the mildest of approaches you might make.
- Blackmail you, by trading on your weaknesses, to do work you shouldn't be doing.
- Subject you to sexual harassment or physical abuse.

The above are just a few of the extreme cases that people have mentioned to me. Such bosses are probably a very small minority, but that's no consolation if one of them is yours.

Possible Remedies
What to do about such bosses? I suppose the ideal answer is to get them before they get you. This may not be easy, but here are some approaches that, between them, may help in dealing with impossible bosses of various kinds:

- Make absolutely sure your boss *knows* how you feel about his or her behaviour. It's just possible that your boss is unaware that you feel badly about it. If so, explain – perhaps putting the emphasis on your feelings rather than on his or her wickedness – e.g. 'I feel really embarrassed when you . . .' rather than 'You've got no right to . . .' (The former is a statement of fact about an outcome, where as the latter states a personal opinion and emphasizes blame. The latter might therefore be seen by your boss as aggressive and might spark off yet more aggression from him or her.)
  Of course, your boss may know only too well how you

feel about his or her behaviour. That may be why he or she does it. In such a case, this approach might not only be pointless but could actually make things worse for you.

- Ensure that all the dealings you have with an impossible boss are recorded in writing – especially if you suspect your boss may deny or distort what has happened or been discussed between you. Send your boss a copy of such a record. And make sure you keep one for yourself in case you are later involved in disciplinary procedures or you wish to pursue your grievance with other people in the organization.

- Discuss your boss with colleagues in your section. Do they feel as badly treated as you do? What, if anything, have they done about it? With what result?

  Do you all feel sufficiently strongly to go and see the boss as a group and present a solid protest?

- Consult your colleagues in informal 'networks' around the organization to learn more about how your boss is seen by others. Do people elsewhere have problems with your boss? Have any of them ever found ways of effectively dealing with his or her undesirable behaviour?

- Consider consulting your boss's boss (provided the two are not in cahoots) – preferably in company with others who feel as you do. If possible, strive to do this in a manner that will be seen as 'attempting to solve a problem for the sake of the organization' rather than 'bolshie workers trying to get rid of a firm boss.'

- If your boss's boss is not to be trusted, consider asking advice from some other influential person with a good reputation in the organization.

- Consider any machinery that exists for lodging an official complaint – e.g. with the Personnel Department. Perhaps the matter will be serious enough for you to start on a 'grievance procedure', if there is any such within your organization. If so, you may be wise to launch this with as little warning as possible so as to avoid your boss getting in first with disciplinary proceedings.

- Consider involving your professional association or trade union. At least, perhaps, ask their advice, even if there is no action they need to or can take.
- Where you believe your boss is offending against the laws of the land (or even just the rules of the organization) – e.g sexual or racial discrimination, health and safety regulations, sexual harassment, fraud – you may need to put a documented case to the highest level of management. Again, this is best done in collaboration with colleagues – the more senior the better.
- In desperation, you may decide to plot with your colleagues to play on your boss's fears or weaknesses in order to bring about his or her exposure and downfall. I have known this be successful on one or two occasions. But it is always a high-risk enterprise. It is more than likely to rebound on the virtuous and well-meaning plotters, leaving the villain unscathed.
- In the end, you may decide that the best way of managing an unmanageable boss is to *leave* him or her – even if you have to take a drop in pay or status going to a more congenial post elsewhere.

☆　☆　☆

I hope you don't feel I am ending this book on too much of a downbeat. But if I'd *started* with unmanageable bosses, I doubt if you'd have read more than the first few pages! Besides, you may be feeling comfortably relaxed in the knowledge that 'My boss can be a bit of a devil sometimes, but at least I don't have problems like those.' And, with luck (and your own good boss –management), you never will. The truly impossible bosses are few and far between – there are probably fewer of them nowadays than there were even twenty or thirty years ago.

No, it is more likely that your continuing problem will be the same one faced by practically all of us who have bosses. How to get a fair deal from a person who is basically decent and reasonable but who will not necessarily act in our best interests unless we keep reminding him or her of what we want and how much he or she will benefit by providing it. In short, just everyday, run-of-the-mill boss management.

POSTSCRIPTS

1. If you happen to be a boss yourself, or get to be one soon, remember that members of your own staff may also have read this book. So please be sympathetic towards their attempts to manage you.

2. Needless to say, I wouldn't pretend to have covered every aspect of the art of boss-management in this short book. If you have any relevant tips or anecdotes that you think might interest readers of the next edition, I'd be very pleased to hear from you (c/o the publishers). Needless to say, in printing any such anecdotes you might tell me about difficult bosses, all names would be changed – to protect the guilty.

STARTING A SMALL BUSINESS

Alan and Deborah Fowler

A Guide to Planning, Finance, Day-to-Day Running and
the Pitfalls to Avoid

* The importance of Product and Market Research
* Legal and Trading Implications
* Preparing Cash Forecasts and Profit Plans
* Patents, Trademarks, Service Marks and Copyright
* Computers: Defining Objectives and Identifying
Software
* Coping with Success – and Dealing with Failure

525 WAYS TO BE A BETTER MANAGER

Ron Coleman & Giles Barrie

When managers fail it's because they don't know how to succeed – not because they've been over-promoted. This book – based on the experience of over 3000 managers – reveals that the key to success lies in learning certain simple skills. In examining the twelve key aspects of management, the authors provide 525 tips that will help you learn these skills.

The areas covered include:
* recruiting and selecting
* maintaining control
* solving people problems
* delegating
* leading and motivating
* managing your own career

Complete with a Personal Action Plan at the end of every chapter, *525 Ways to be a Better Manager* is the complete, comprehensive guide to effective action – whether you are already a managing director or still hoping for your first promotion.

BEWARE THE NAKED MAN WHO OFFERS YOU HIS SHIRT

Harvey Mackay

Brilliant, brief and biting, here are more golden nuggets of business wisdom from the author of the sensational international bestseller *Swim with the Sharks Without Being Eaten Alive*.

But this time there is much, much more. This book is nothing less than a roadmap for your career. Whether you're just starting out, or anywhere along the journey, it will help you make the most of every working moment. You'll be able to:

* 'Take this job and love it'
* Add the missing ingredient – courage – to your career
* Learn secrets on servicing sales worth millions
* Develop can't-miss strategies for getting a rise
* Find out why caring is contagious
* Work out how to satisfy everyone – employers *and* employees

And that's not all. There is a questionnaire that could revolutionize your management style, a self-inventory and corporate climate test and, in case the bad guys get you down, a sure-fire strategy for fighting back . . .

☐	Starting a Small Business	Alan & Deborah Fowler	£5.99
☐	Your Business Handbook	Alan & Deborah Fowler	£14.99
☐	525 Ways to be a Better Manager	Ron Coleman & Giles Barrie	£6.99
☐	Swim With the Sharks	Harvey Mackay	£4.99
☐	Beware the Naked Man Who Offers You His Shirt	Harvey Mackay	£6.99
☐	Innovator's Handbook	Vincent Nolan	£9.99
☐	The Manager's Handbook	Arthur Young	£14.99
☐	The Manager's Problem Solver	John Walsh	£14.99

Warner Books now offers an exciting range of quality titles by both established and new authors. All of the books in this series are available from:

Little, Brown and Company (UK) Limited,
P.O. Box 11,
Falmouth,
Cornwall TR10 9EN.

Alternatively you may fax your order to the above address. Fax No. 0326 376423.

Payments can be made as follows: cheque, postal order (payable to Little, Brown and Company) or by credit cards, Visa/Access. Do not send cash or currency. UK customers and B.F.P.O. please allow £1.00 for postage and packing for the first book, plus 50p for the second book, plus 30p for each additional book up to a maximum charge of £3.00 (7 books plus).

Overseas customers including Ireland, please allow £2.00 for the first book plus £1.00 for the second book, plus 50p for each additional book.

NAME (Block Letters) ....

....

ADDRESS ....

....

....

☐ I enclose my remittance for _____

☐ I wish to pay by Access/Visa Card

Number ☐☐☐☐☐☐☐☐☐☐☐☐☐☐☐☐

Card Expiry Date ☐☐☐☐